Dr. Sharifah bint Mohammad bin Nasir Al-Oboudi, a writer, novelist, and freelance researcher, has a PhD degree from Alexandria University. Published, in Arabic, three novels, a short story collection, and a book on literary criticism. Also published two scholarly articles on the history of Najd, the heart of Arabia. Al-Oboudi writes on new findings in nutrition.

Dr. Sharifah bint Mohammad binNasir Al-Oboudi

Narrative Techniques in the Book of The Thousand and One Nights

And Its Impact on World Fiction

AUSTIN MACAULEY PUBLISHERS™

LONDON * CAMBRIDGE * NEW YORK * SHARJAH

ISBN – 9789948844624 – (Paperback)
ISBN – 9789948844617 – (E-Book)

Application Number: MC-10-01-9043165
Age Classification: 17+

Printer Name: iPrint Global Ltd
Printer Address: Witchford, England

First Published (2021)
AUSTIN MACAULEY PUBLISHERS FZE
Sharjah Publishing City
P.O Box [519201]
Sharjah, UAE
www.austinmacauley.ae
+971 655 95 202

Narrative Techniques in the Book of The Thousand and One Nights and its Impact on World Fiction is based on my PhD dissertation with the title: *Metafiction and John Barth's The Book of Ten Nights and a Night: Eleven Stories and Naguib Mahfouz's Arabian Nights and Days.*

My dissertation is a shared project that has depended on individual effort as well as on professional guidance and emotional support. My success in completing my dissertation is largely due to those who have guided and inspired me all the way through. I deeply thank Professor Sahar Hamouda for her long and demanding, although enjoyable, journey with me in the process of shaping this work. Her intellectual insight, professional expertise, and constant encouragement have pushed me forward to the final product. I also deeply thank Professor Azza Mohamed Helmy el-Kholy for her careful reading and constructive criticism of my work. I am also grateful to the Department of English Language and Literature, Faculty of Arts, Alexandria University for their support and encouragements.

My deepest gratitude goes to my family members; first of all to my mother, Nora Al Odhaib, my father, Mohammad Al Oboudi, my daughters and sons, and all my brothers and sisters for their confidence in my abilities and constant encouragements. Second, I particularly appreciate the continuous support of my husband Mohammad Al Maarik who has always been proud of me and of my achievements. He has provided me with everything he could to help me finish my dissertation.

Table of contents

Preface

The marvelous book *The Book of The Thousand and One Nights* has been an enchanting literary construct for its narrative techniques and timeless appeal. *The Nights*[1] has an interesting history, and its translation into European languages has affected major literary figures throughout the ages. Chapter I of this book deals with the history of *The Nights* and how it has reached the West and affected the literary imagination in the West during the eighteenth century, which is considered the starting point of the beginning of literary theory. Chapter I also demonstrates how the numerous translations of *The Nights* have created not only one text but also several different texts colored by intentions, angles of vision of their translators, and degrees of deviation from the original text. These translated texts, which have been sources of inspiration that helped shape the consciousness of literary figures from the eighteenth century on, contain slightly different narrative techniques depending on faithfulness of translation to the original version or versions.

The Nights consists of a framed collection of stories that rely on story-telling for their presentation. *The Nights* is fiction about fiction, stories about story-telling; it is metafiction that abandons reality through stressing its fictionality by the very nature of story-telling. Yet, Shahrazad's so-called reality of facing death every night is manipulated to introduce that fictionality. So, the over repetition of the main covert reason for telling the tales of *The Nights* creates a sense of illusion that shakes the steadiness of the text as a whole. In addition, as in metafiction, there are intertextual references to a story or stories in every night of story-telling, where the system of their fictionality is reworked and rechecked on each and every night. There is self-reference to previously known stories from Mesopotamia, India, Persia, and Arabia throughout *The Nights*. This classic contains a huge number of stories within stories of imaginary characters: ginn, sages, speaking animals, and exotic surroundings that assert its fictionality.

Moreover, Shahrazad[2], the main narrator of *The Nights*, is completely involved in the fictional setting because her life is at stake if she does not

---

[1] From here on, *The Book of the Thousand and One Nights* will be referred to as *The Nights* unless the content requires otherwise.

[2] Spelling of names and words of Eastern origin such as Shahrazad, Shahrayar, wazir, and genni or ginn vary in accordance with sources or versions of *The Nights*. In this book, I adopt Sir Richard Burton's spelling style found in *The Thousand and One Night* as he, in his preface to *The Nights* says, "As words are the embodiment of ideas and writing is of words, so the word is the spoken word; and we should write it as pronounced… In all

continue to narrate! Shahrazad comments on her stories addressing her father the wazir, and her king Shahrayar among many others. Shahrazad intrudes to interrupt the flow of narration when necessary or cut it altogether at the approach of dawn. These characteristics of *The Nights* are the same characteristics of metafiction in literature that keep attracting writers of fiction such as Jorge Luis Borges, Naguib Mahfouz, and John Barth over and over again. It is important to mention that several factors such as Globalization, Orientalism, Chaos Theory, and the different translations of *The Nights* that created different texts which have been received differently have changed the way readers receive *The Nights*.

Chapter II of this book gets out of *The Nights* but delves into the history and source of experimentation in writing fiction. Starting in the 1960s, many writers of fiction left conventional writing techniques of realism and modernism to engage in styles of writing that celebrate the increased awareness of personal, social, and cultural self-consciousness. From that period on, most critics and theoreticians have considered this shift to experimentation as a novel form of expression and a new phenomenon called metafiction. Metafiction itself is a broad term that covers a wide range of literary techniques that reveal literary creativity, extreme self-consciousness of the writing process, and reference to other known works of art as a form of self-reflexivity. The literary techniques of metafiction have been theorized, in general, as postmodern phenomena and products of the period around the 1960s. This is not to imply that some metafictional techniques did not occur in earlier Western fiction, but it is logical to say that the 1960s and 70s represent the times of the flourish of metafiction.

However, a number of scholars have been taking the start of metafiction to much earlier periods. These scholars, such as Robert Scholes, Linda Hutcheon, Larry McCaffrey, and Ihab Hassan do not limit metafiction to the contemporary period of postmodernism, but none of them provides a study of *The Nights* as an early example of a metafictional work. Literary works with narrative techniques of metafiction (even though these works may not be acknowledged as having metafictional techniques) have, therefore, intrigued literary tastes for a long time. These works range from the pre-modernist period, such as *The Nights*, to modernist works such as James Joyce's *Finnegans Wake*, to contemporary works

---

tongues vowel-sounds, the flesh which clothes the bones (consonants) of language, are affected by the consonants which precede and more especially which follow them, hardening and softening the articulation; and deeper sounds accompany certain letters." (xxxix).

With respect to proper names and untranslated Arabic words, Burton says on the same page that he has "rejected all system in favour of common sense." In cases of incorporating terms into English, Burton refuses to "follow the purist and mortify the reader by startling innovation." For instance, Burton thinks that Aleppo, Cairo, and Bassorah are preferred to a more correct Halab, Kahirah, and Al–Basrah. Also, when a word is half-naturalized, as he says, like alcoran or Koran, Bashwa or Pasha; and Mahomet or Mohammed (for Muhammad), the modern form is adopted because it has become more familiar. But, [Burton adds] I see no advantage in retaining them simply because they are the mistakes of a past generation" (xxix-xl). Spelling of names of Eastern origin will stay as is if they appear in a quotation.

that belong to the postmodern era and after, such as Naguib Mahfouz's *Arabian Nights and Days* and John Barth's *Book of Ten Nights and a Night: Eleven Stories*[3].

In order to comprehend the impact of Metafiction on literature and on the progress of literary theory, this book finds it important to include a whole chapter on the analysis of metafiction, the highlight of experimentation in fiction, by explaining its techniques and defining how the term has originated and how it has been theorized following its extensive technical application in works of fiction from the 1960s on. This chapter also registers opinions of literary critics who associate the rise of metafiction with cultural and intellectual changes the West went through after World War II. In addition, Chapter discusses other critics who broaden the scope of the application of metafictional techniques by briefly referring to works of fiction that predate World War II and that obviously contain metafictional elements.

The roots of metafiction, as this book tries to prove, are, in fact, located in a well-known work from a period that even preceded realism and modernism as periods. *The Nights* has obvious characteristics of metafiction. However, the West has been overlooking this famous work as the source of metafiction probably because *The Nights* is not part of the Western literary canon. However, several factors have been drawing attention to *The Nights* as a source of literary experimentation or metafiction. First, the engagements of John Barth, one of the most successful literary experimentalists, with *The Nights* since the late 1960s forcefully draw attention to this famous work of art as one of the clearest examples of what metafiction is all about. Second, more studies concerning narrative techniques in *The Nights* have been increasingly conducted[4] in the West during the last few decades. Third, newly emerging factors such as globalization, interest in Orientalism, and chaos theory have helped in defining the applications of metafictional techniques as literature in general and metafiction in particular can be viewed as a mirror that reflects changes societies undergo. All these factors direct attention to *The Nights* as one of the earliest sources of metafiction.

Chapter III analyzes Naguib Mahfouz's metafictional novel, *Arabian Nights and Days*. Mahfouz's novel is included in this book because it is a contemporary text strongly connected to the original, *The Nights*, and it questions the purpose

---

[3] The book of *Ten Nights and a Night: Eleven Stories* will be referred to from here on as *Ten Nights* unless the content requires otherwise.

[4] Studies and references to *The Nights* started in the twentieth century with Borges' works, continued with Barth's interest in this classic, and appeared in such works as Ferial Ghazoul's *The Arabian Nights: A Structural Analysis* (1980) and her other work *Nocturnal Poetics: The Arabian Nights in Comparative Context* (1996), Salman Rushdie's *The Sea of Stories* (1990), David Pinault's *Story-Telling Techniques in The Arabian Nights* (1992), A. S. Byatt's *The Djinn in the Nightingale's Eye* (1994), Robert Irwin's *The Arabian Nights: A Companion* (1994), Eva Sallis' *Scheherazade Through the Looking Glass: The Metamorphosis of The Thousand and One Nights* (1999), Luis Paulo Parreiras-Horta's dissertation *Mirrors of Ink and Wonderful Lamps: The Arabian Nights in Victorian and Postmodern Literature* (2004), plus numerous articles published in scholarly journals.

behind stories and story-telling. It is here precisely where Mahfouz and Barth do meet. Chapter IV proposes that Mahfouz's novel is an important building block of contemporary metafiction because it represents a continuation of the 'art of nights,' which in itself is a form of metafictional technique in its insistence on story-telling. This metafictional art started with the original *Nights* narratives, and continued in other well-known works from Edgar Allan Poe's short story "The Thousand and Second Tale of Scheherazade" to John Barth's 2004 *Ten Nights*, and will probably generate more future inspirations as the popularity of the original *Nights* is not declining but increasing.

Mahfouz's novel, published in 1979 in Arabic and translated into English in 1995, has similarities and differences with the original, *The Nights*. Mahfouz's novel has the same central characters: Shahrazad, Shahrayar, the wazir etc., and the same continuation of 'the art of nights' through the enchanting and inviting title. Nevertheless, Mahfouz's Shahrazad is not the story-teller but, like all the characters in the novel, she is introduced by the omniscient narrator. More importantly, Mahfouz's novel starts at the thousand and second night of story-telling when Shahrayar, fulfilled by story-telling, decides to spare the life of Shahrazad and accept her as his wife. Mahfouz's novel goes beyond the original, *The Nights*, in that Mahfouz's Shahrayar "slowly learns about justice and mercy, the Angel of Death [the character who represents death according to Byatt] is a bric-a-brac merchant, and genies play tricks with fate."[5] Mahfouz's novel is a self-reflexive metafictional novel with ancient characters that are, in a way, tied to the present turmoil of the political situation of the Middle East. Mahfouz's work is a "collection of magical tales, with a political edge and a spiritual depth."[6] It is a metafictional work that views realities through fiction. Again, globalization, Orientalism, and social and political world events have participated in spreading the effect of Mahfouz's novel beyond the boundaries of Egypt which also show interaction between West and East.

Chapter IV reveals how the metafictionist John Barth has been exploiting Shahrazad and her framed stories while he has been practically participating in theorizing contemporary metafiction and shaping contemporary literary theory.[7] Jorge Luis Borges and John Barth are the two most important contemporary literary figures who recognized *The Nights* and its distinctive narrative style in more than one of their creative and critical works. However, neither of them has explicitly recognized the affinities between *The Nights* and metafiction. John Barth in particular has devoted a large sum of his metafiction to the celebration of Shahrazad and *The Nights*. Barth's reasons for this devotion lie in the fact that he has found in *The Nights* a bottomless source of narrative inspiration. Chapter

---

[5] A. S. Byatt "The Greatest Story Ever Told" xix. Byatt has two articles exploring The Nights "The Greatest Story Ever Told" (2000), and "Narrate or Die" (2004). The two articles are the same except that the second is an elaboration of the first.

[6] Byatt "The Greatest Story Ever Told" xix

[7] John Barth's tremendous amount of fiction employing *The Nights* and his numerous essays collected in his books, *The Friday Book* and *Further Fridays*, acknowledging *The Nights* forcefully draw attention to him in any study of this classic.

III tries to prove the idea that Barth goes even further in his devotion to *The Nights* by being influenced by another contemporary *Nights*: Naguib Mahfouz's *The Arabian Nights and Days*. Mahfouz's novel goes beyond the relatively narrow stream of politics and into the wide river of the value of literature and story-telling. Both this political edge and its story-telling value also exist in John Barth's 2004 collection, *Ten Nights*. Barth's first sentence goes, "There was meant to have been a book called *Ten Nights and a Night*, which, had it gotten itself written before TEOTWAE(A)KI 9/11/2001-The End Of The World As We (Americans) Knew it…" (*Ten Nights* 1). There are general characteristics that tie Barth's collection, *Ten Nights* to the original *Nights*. Barth's metafictional work is self-reflexive of 'the art of nights.' As with the original *Nights* that contains previously known tales, Barth's tales are pieces that are previously and independently published but never in a collection. In addition, instead of a thousand and one nights of story-telling, Barth's creation stretches across a time span of eleven nights only with the number eleven having connotations of political implications. Moreover, it is not Shahrazad that narrates and Shahrayar that listens but Graybard the old teller with the muse WYSIWYG: What You See Is What You Get inspiring his stories. Furthermore, the frame narrative of Barth's collection moves away from that of the original *The Nights* and gets closer to Naguib Mahfouz's theme in *Arabian Nights and Days*.

Chapter IV concludes by addressing how Barth's vast knowledge of newly emerging factors such as globalization, Orientalism, and chaos theory have been incorporated into his fiction and non-fiction works. Along with his concentration on exploring not only *The Nights* but also relatively all major world's literary classics, Barth has always been quick in adopting whatever changes happen in the world into his canon. Interaction between West and East could also be traced through the analysis of trends or changes in his work.

The conclusion of this book stresses the point of proposing a wider literary theory that stops relating metafiction to the postmodernism of the 1960s and 70s and starts relating metafiction to *The Nights*. The book, therefore, is an attempt to find the exact nature of metafiction and the interaction that resulted from its production back and forth between East and West. It is also an attempt to find the exact location of the metafictionality of Barth's *Ten Nights* between the original, *The Nights*, and Mahfouz's *Arabian Nights and Days*, in order to show that fiction produced in the East is still active and capable of drawing the attention of major literary figures. This book is also an attempt to include not only the original, *The Nights*, but also Mahfouz's *Arabian Nights and Days* as representative examples of metafiction and as building blocks that contribute to the development of metafiction and literary theory. The title of my study reflects, I hope, the relation the three works (*The Nights*, Barth's *Ten Nights,* and Mahfouz's *Arabian Nights and Days*) have with each other and with metafiction.

Chapter I

The Book of The Thousand And One Nights And Its Narrative Techniques

كتاب ألف ليلة و ليلة و ألف ليلة و ليلة Kitab alf laylah wa laylah (in Arabic), *The Book of One Thousand and One Nights, The One Thousand and One Nights, The Thousand and One Nights, The Book of a Thousand Nights and a Night, The 1001 Nights, The Arabian Nights*, Les Mille et une nuits (in French), are all titles for the same literary work known and admired all over the world for centuries. The tremendous impact of this fascinating world classic could be seen not only on shaping the imagination of writers of literature, which is reflected in their work, but also on the direction literary theory, in general, has been taking. In order to show such a tremendous impact, this chapter will give first a briefing on the history of this work and the writers who have been most influenced by it. More importantly, this chapter will then explain the metafictional elements that are essential to *The Nights* long before this term (metafiction) was coined sometime during the second half of the twentieth century. The origin of metafiction was unjustly related to the postmodern era of the 1960s and the 1970s or even earlier but not early enough to reach *The Nights*. To do justice to *The Nights*, this chapter undertakes the task of explaining the striking affinities between *The Nights* and what metafiction is all about which will be done, first of all, through shedding some light on the history of this literary creation and the writers most affected by it. The history of the formation of *The Nights* provides information on the diverse sources of narratives constituting this classic, and it highlights its fragmented nature; Diversity and fragmentation in narratives are characteristic of metafiction. Also, concentrating on the huge number of writers affected by *The Nights* is purposely done to direct attention to its tremendous impact on world literature in relation to its seclusion from literary theory.

In brief, the history of *The Nights* is, I believe, the history of man on Earth since the origins of the tales making up *The Nights* are almost untraceable. In this classic work, there are tales, myths, and folk stories from ancient Mesopotamia, Syria, Egypt, India, Persia, and Yemen. The role of the Muslim Arabs in the creation of this marvelous work resembles their role in human history. In human history, the Arabs took past knowledge from various sources, as did all great civilizations, polished that knowledge, added to it, improved upon it, preserved it, and handed it down to people who led the world after them. In the case of *The Nights*, the Arabs collected a huge number of tales from various sources and civilizations, adopted, probably from Persia or through Persia, a frame story for the presentation of these tales, and gave the collection a fascinating title that indicates the infinity of the relationship between fiction and reality.

Although the original Arabic manuscript of this world classic has never been located, the adaptation and translation of the Persian frame story of Shahrayar and Shahrazad, called "Hazar Afsana" (in Persian) which means a thousand legends and the addition and Arabization of a number of Indian tales happened in Baghdad or Basra probably as early as the 8th century Gregorian that corresponds to the 2nd century Hejrah as Eva Sallis says:

> "The 9th/3rd centuries fragment of The *Thousand Nights* made famous by Nabia Abbott in 1949Gregorian/1368 Hijri is the earliest extant piece of information available on the history of the *Nights* and, interestingly, also the earliest known portion of a paper book."[8]

During the 9th century, reference to this classic appears in several sources, the most important of which are *The Fihrist* (catalogue of books) by Mohammad Ibn Al Nadim which includes a brief history of *The Nights* as a book and mentions its Persian origin as *Hazar Afsana*[9]. Ibn Al Nadim says that "although *Hazar Afsana* means 'A Thousand Nights,' there were only about 200 stories in the collection"[10]. Roughly at the same period, the book *Morouj Al Thahab* (Meadows of Gold) by Ali Ibn Husain Al Mas'udi also mentions *The Nights* as a book of tales of Persian and Indian origins. However, Robert Irwin says that Silvestre de Sacy, a great linguist and expert editor of texts who published a review of the Calcutta 1 edition of *The Nights*, "offhandedly discounted the evidence from Al-Mas'udi that the stories had a Persian and, ultimately, an Indian source."[11] Irwin says the stories seem to de Sacy "too Arab and too Islamic ever to have come from India."[12]

> Irwin also says that Ibn Al Nadim and Al Masu'di were always inclined to ascribe a Persian or an Indian origin to works of fiction. Often they were right to do so. However, in the case of the important *Sindibadnama* cycle of stories, [which is of Syriac origin] al-Masu'di's belief that they had an Indian origin led nineteenth-century scholars...to look in the wrong direction.[13]

To add even more to the confusion, Irwin mentions that the writer of a late-eighteenth-century Turkish story collection with the title *Phantasm of the Divine Presence* has in its preface that Ali Aziz Efendi the Cretan claims to be

---

[8] Eva Sallis 19
[9] Husain Haddawy xiv, Irwin 51
[10] Robert Irwin *Companion* 50
[11] Irwin *Companion* 44
[12] Irwin *Companion* 44
[13] Irwin *Companion* 75

translating from, among other sources, *Elf Leyle* (i.e. '*The Thousand Nights*') by al-Asma'i. Ali's story collection does indeed contain versions of stories that are common to the *Arabic Nights*, but he provides no supporting evidence that al-Asma'i, the distinguished ninth-century Basran philologist and companion of the Caliph Harun al-Rashid, did indeed compile such a collection; and in general, scholars have been chary of attributing the *Nights* to a single author.[14]

In light of this information, the nuclei of many of the stories, in my opinion, have probably originated somewhere in ancient Egypt, Mesopotamia, and/or Syria far back in history before the Greek, Persian, or Indian civilization were formed. Greece, Persia, and India were stations where these stories landed for a while, then the stories were transmitted to another flourishing civilization. The reason behind such speculation is the continuous discoveries of historical cuneiforms of literary nature in present day Egypt (the Story of Sinuhe or the Westcar Papyrus), in Iraq (The Gilgamesh Epic), and in Syria (The Ugarit wealth of epics, poetry, and stories). These findings reveal that narration has always been an important part in human civilizations at their heights. To be more precise, "the 'tale of Hasib' in night 482, where the wise Daniyal prays to God to have a son can be traced to the epic of Baal from the Ugarit civilization from the fourteenth century BC."[15] Throughout the ages and up until the present time, *The Nights* has become a very long book with numerous versions translated into several languages. These versions contain different numbers of stories and tales, but all share the same frame story of Shahrazad telling stories to King Shahrayar.

Even though "the history of textual transmission of *The Nights* has been muddied by forgers and compilers of pastiche manuscripts of the stories,"[16] one thing remains which is the frame story of the ordeal of Shahrayar and the brave and intelligent Shahrazad telling stories to save her life. This frame story acquired universality as "Scheherazade's tales have lived on, like germ cells, in many literatures."[17] Although the oldest reference to *The Nights* as a book contains the same frame story of Shahrayar and Shahrazad, "there is no evidence that the 9th/3rd century version contains the same stories and tales as the modern versions have."[18] Nevertheless, whatever the origin and number of stories in each version, "the tales themselves promise to be timeless and free of all frontiers. For they form, let it be said boldly, the world greatest single treasure house of fiction, and their riches are for all men."[19] All in all, *The Nights*, according to Irwin in his book *The Arabian Nights: A Companion* contains fairy tales, long heroic epics, wisdom literature, fables, cosmological fantasy, pornography, scatological jokes, mystical devotional tales, chronicles of low life, rhetorical debates, and masses of poetry.[20] This vast body of literature or literary related items is an

---

[14] Irwin *Companion* 50
[15] Stanislav Segert 108
[16] Irwin *Companion* 42
[17] A. S. Byatt "Narrate or Die" xvii
[18] N. J. Dawood 8
[19] Ben Ray Redman viii
[20] Irwin *Companion* 2

important indication of the precedence of *The Nights* as a creative work of fiction.

The title of *The Thousand and One Nights*, or the addition of a night to the thousand ones in the title, first appeared in Al Mas'udi's reference to this work as he says that "the people call it 'A Thousand and One Nights.'"[21] However, Robert Irwin disagrees with taking the additional night far back in time as he says, "there was certainly a version of the story collection circulating in the tenth century (though it was entitled *The Thousand Nights*, not *The Thousand and One Nights*)."[22] What is important is that the addition of a night to the already large and figurative number of a thousand is an important step in the narrative path. It symbolizes infinity and directs attention to the nature of the book itself, *The Nights*, as a collection of narratives reflecting vast human knowledge and experience.

The development of this treasure continued with time, and "the Arab *rawis* or professional story-tellers knew how to add local coloring to the foreign tale and how to adapt it to native surroundings"[23] giving more Arabic and Islamic flavors that have remained with *The Nights* ever since. However, it is hard to follow changes that occurred to *The Nights*, but the presence of the 14th century manuscript located now in Paris, France, indicates "the definitive compilation of the corpus and its final recording."[24] This, however, does not mean that there was no other written version or versions before then, as it is well-documented in history that the Mongols burned Baghdad and its libraries during the thirteenth century, which may point to a loss of earlier versions. The 14th century manuscript "has come to be regarded as the 'standard' text of the *Nights*."[25] This earliest Arabic manuscript, which contains about 300 tales and is located in the National Library in Paris, France, reveals that more stories and tales, valuable or less valuable, have been added to *The Nights* in order to reach the number of 1001. Changes (addition/omission of stories and tales) that happened to *The Nights* after the so-called original manuscript are indicative, in my opinion, of the nature of *The Nights* as a literary work reflective of the culture that produced it. *The Nights*, in its diverse Arabic versions (or numerous printed translations later on), is a flexible unique work capable of adapting to the needs and demands of the culture that takes it into its realm. All versions share, with few exceptions, the following stories: The Merchant and the Demon (with two or three enframed tales), The Fisherman and the Demon (with two enframed tales),The Story of the Porter and the Three Ladies (with five tales), The Hunchback cycle, including the stories of The Barber and his Six Brothers, The Story of the Three Apples, enframing The Story of the Wazirs Nur al-Din and Shams al-Din, The Story of Nur al-Din Ali and Anis al-Jalis, The Story of Ali Ibn Baqqar and Shams al-Nahar, and The Story of Qamar al-Zaman. It is important to note that titles of

---

[21] Dawood 8

[22] Irwin *Companion* 4

[23] Dawood 8

[24] Andre Miquel 7

[25] Dawood 8

stories sometimes change due to variations in pronunciations and translations. For instance, The Merchant and the Demon is called The Merchant and the Jinnee or the Djinn in some versions.

In print, the first printed Arabic edition of *The Nights* is the 1814/1229 and 1818/1233 two-volume Calcutta I, edited by Sheikh Ahmad Ibn Mahmud Shirwani Al Yamani, and it contains two hundred nights and the story of Sinbad the sailor. "He pieced this edition together from a late Syrian manuscript and a work containing classical anecdotes, choosing the texts at random… He edited as he pleased."[26] Robert Irwin believes that Shirwani, a teacher of Arabic, intended the text to be used by learners of Arabic.[27]

The second printed edition is the 1825/1240–1838/1259 twelve-volume Breslau of Maximilian Habicht and Heinrich Fleischer edition (eight edited by Habicht and four by Fleischer) in collaboration with Murad Al Najjar. This text of 1001 tales is a compilation from Syrian and Egyptian sources.

The third printed edition is the 1835/1251 Bulaq or Cairo edition which is also in two volumes. It is the first non-European version of *The Nights* printed by the Egyptian government, and it contains one thousand and one nights of story-telling. Due to its length maybe, Eva Sallis says that this edition "is not a faithful transcription of its sources."[28] On the other hand, Irwin says, "the Bulaq text does not look like a composite one. Rather, it is thought to have been based on a single Egyptian manuscript of the eighteenth century, now lost."[29] Again, the Bulaq edition is, I believe, another legitimate version that reveals, more than other versions, the character of the Egyptian culture.

The fourth printed version is the 1839/1255–1842/1258 four-volume Calcutta II or W. H. Macnaghten edition that resembles the Bulaq edition in that it contains 190 main stories, some of which have an Egyptian flavor. The Bulaq and the Macnaghten editions "formed, and for many still represent, the standard *Nights* text"[30] as the two carry both Syrian and Egyptian traits. Before these editions, the tales of *The Nights* in Arabic were believed to be orally circulating for centuries in the Arab World in a close-to-colloquial language by unknown authors where the stories of Shahrazad and Shahrayar were considered parts of literary folklore.

Interest in *The Nights* in the Arab World continued during the twentieth century where several Arabic texts of *The Nights* were published. In 1954, N. J. Dawood published a translation after he noticed that "the average English reader's acquaintance with the *Nights* begins and ends with the nursery adaptations."[31] Dawood justifies a need for a fresh translation of the best of *The Nights* stories, as he says that there is a need for a readable version.[32] In 1984,

---

[26] Haddawy xvii

[27] Irwin *Companion* 43

[28] Eva Sallis 30

[29] Irwin *Companion* 44

[30] Sallis 30

[31] Dawood 10

[32] Dawood 10

Muhsin Mahdi produced a version titled *Alf Layla Wa Layla*, which he says is compiled from the fourteenth century manuscript that had been used by Galland. According to Irwin, Mahdi "was able to offer some plausible speculations about the circumstances of composition of the original or 'mother' source (in Arabic, *al-nuskha al-umm)* from which the archetype derived."[33] It suffices to belief that "Mahdi has produced an authentic medieval text available to Arabists who are interested in the language, style, and narrative technique of the *Nights.*"[34] However, Irwin criticizes Mahdi for his neglect of the late longer Egyptian version as he depends heavily on manuscripts in European libraries collected by European travelers; Irwin discusses the matter fully and arrives at a conclusion that the Egyptian version was based on a fuller source.[35] Once again, critics' acceptance of more than an authentic version of *The Nights* is a proof of the open-endedness and flexibility of this classic.

In Europe, it is common knowledge that "individual stories from the *Nights* had been included in medieval and Renaissance story collections."[36] For example, "The Merchant and the Two Sharpers" that appears in *The Nights* has strong similarities with the story of "The Pardoner's Tale" in *The Canterbury Tales*; the Ebony Horse in *The Nights* is very similar to the one in Chaucer's "The Squire's Tale."[37] It is interesting to note that the first printed version of *The Nights* was a French translation from Arabic done by Abbé Antoine Galland whose translation became a base for other subsequent French, German, and English translations of this famous work. Galland's twelve-volume *Les Mille et une nuits* which was published from 1704/1116 to 1716/1129, relied on a four-volume Arabic manuscript now available in the Bibliotheque Nationale in Paris. Muhsin Mahdi in his editing of Galland's translation mentions that Galland's translation includes 40 stories narrated over 282 nights; these were available in the early Mamluke period and written down in Syria.[38] However, Galland's translation[39] is not a literal translation as he worked on the stories to fit contemporary European tastes. Galland worked on *The Nights* "emphasizing the fantastic and the miraculous and carefully avoiding the candid references to sex."[40] To that, it has been believed that Galland added other famous tales that were not parts of the original manuscript but told to Galland by a Syrian friend, Hanna Diab, such as "Aladdin and the Magic Lamp" and "Ali Baba and the Forty Thieves."

In 1706/1118, the first English version of *The Nights* appeared. It was "a Grub Street English version [that] went into many editions, and was itself followed by other translations, pseudo-translations, and imitations, so numerous

---

[33] Irwin *Companion* 55
[34] Irwin 55–56, Haddawy xxiii
[35] Irwin *Companion* 60
[36] Irwin *Companion* 42
[37] Irwin *Companion* 63–64
[38] Irwin *Companion* 57
[39] According to Haddawy xix, and Dawood 9
[40] Dawood 9

that by 1800 there were more than eighty such collections."[41] These versions, although not of high quality, had delighted the English Romantics in their childhood and enflamed their imagination.[42]

The next text was by Henry Torrens who published a literal incomplete translation (1838/1254) of only the first fifty of the original nights. Edward William Lane followed by translating a three-volume version (1838/1254) derived from the Bulaq edition. Lane's translation contains the frame story and a small number of tales that fitted the conservative English taste of the period. It was Lane who started the fashion of adding notes to the translation as travel to the East and knowledge about it were popular at that time. "His work is presented as information for the scholar and gentleman, rather than entertainment for the people in general… His translation is direct and clear in style, though, very sadly, heavily edited and even bowdlerized."[43]

John Payne followed in about 1882/1300 with a complete nine-volume translation that "draws mainly from the Macnaghten edition but supplemented from the Bulaq and other texts."[44] Even though Payne's translation preceded Burton's translation by about two years, it did not acquire the same fame that Burton's translation acquired simply because it appeared in a limited edition of 500 copies only. Payne's translation, like Burton's, uses a pseudo-archaic style. This is one of the reasons Burton was accused of plagiarizing Payne's work, but it remains that "Payne's is the better translation, being slightly easier for the contemporary reader and being the source for a substantial part of Burton's but, owing to undeserved obscurity, it is now extremely rare."[45]

Sir Richard Burton came next (1884/1302) with a completed ten-volume translation (plus six, and some say seven, supplemental volumes) which became the most famous English version. Burton, who spoke more than 35 languages, is highly conscious of the value of the source language of his translation to the extent that "he tried to invent an English version of mediaeval Arabic, drawing on Chaucer, Elizabethan English…"[46] Burton's translation is more than a translation as he tried to capture the spirit of *The Nights* by preserving the poetic nature of Arabic and by loading his translation with explanations in the form of notes. Burton's translation has its admirers and detractors. Borges says, "Burton combines many readings and many writings, and something of his own fierce dynamism and elaborate intricacy."[47] Another admirer Redman says:

"Whatever the virtues or faults of Burton's cragged, highly idiosyncratic style, he was temperamentally closer to the *nights* themselves than any other of their Western interpreters. Not only was he an Orientalist of wide and precise knowledge; he was almost an Oriental. So far as an Englishman could, he

---

[41] Haddawy xx

[42] Dawood 9; Sallis 3; Haddawy xx

[43] Sallis 3

[44] Sallis 4

[45] Sallis 4

[46] Byatt "Narrate or Die" xvi

[47] Byatt "Narrate or Die" xvii

identified himself with the Moslim [sic] East and its people, lived their life, thought their thoughts, and absorbed their racial past in his own alien consciousness."[48]

On the other hand, there is Robert Irwin who claims that the heavy-handedness of Burton's translation "made him want to slit his throat,"[49] as what "Burton gained in accuracy he lost in style. His excessive weakness for the archaic, his habit of coining words and phrases, and the unnatural idiom he affected, detract from the literary quality of his translation."[50] In spite of all opinions, Burton's translation was very successful in capturing and enriching the imagination of Victorian England.

The French version of J. C. Mardrus's appeared in 1899/1317, which he claimed was an accurate and scholarly one. This version was taken by Powys Mathers and translated into English. "Ironically, most people who have read a complete version of the *Nights* have read this misleading translation, for it is readily available."[51] Mardrus's translation is thought to be misleading because it presents the East as a far more exotic place than it really was.

Enno Littmann translated and edited a scholarly German edition in six volumes; a version that is "literal but without literary charm."[52] Other German versions, one by Henning, and another by Weil, were also produced. In Spanish, a version by Cansinos-Assens was produced which Borges thinks excellent.

All these translations, and before them all Arabic manuscripts or individual stories that authors of fiction have come across, have had a profound impact in shaping the narrative consciousness in the West, and from the moment Galland translated *The Nights*, literature in Europe acquired new dimensions. In his book, *The Arabian Nights: A Companion*, Robert Irwin devotes a full chapter, "Children of the Nights," to the influence of this classic upon Western authors of fiction and says:

"From the eighteenth century onwards, translations of the *Nights* circulated so widely in Europe and America that to ask about its influence on Western literature is a little like asking about the influence on Western literature of that other great collection of oriental tales, the Bible."[53]

In his *Companion*, Irwin gives a chronological order of authors' names and literary works that show the influence of *The Nights*. The most famous of these authors and their works are Anthony Hamilton's *Histoire du Fleur d'Epine*, (*The Story of May-flower*); Crebillon Fils's *Le Sopha*; Denis Diderot's *Les Bijoux indiscrets*; Montesquieu's *Les Lettres persanes*; Jacques Cazotte's *La Patte du chat*, and his parody of *The Nights*: *Les Mille et une Fadaises*; and Voltaire's *Zadiq ou la destine* and *Candide*. "It has been estimated that almost 700

---

[48] Redman xii
[49] Byatt "Narrate or Die" xvi
[50] Dawood 10
[51] Sallis 4
[52] Borges *The Thousand and One Nights* 55
[53] Irwin *Companion* 273

romances in the oriental mode were published in France in the eighteenth century."[54]

In England, writings with oriental flavor also spread. John Hawkesworth produced *Almoran and Hamet*; James Ridley published *Tales of the Ginii, or the Delightful Lessons of Horan, the Son of Asmar*; Frances Sheridan wrote *Nourjahad*; Clara Reeve wrote *The History of Charoba, Queen of Egypt*; William Beckford produced his masterpiece, *Vathek*, which, according to Irwin, influenced Byron, Disraeli, Poe, Melville and Lovecraft.[55]

In the nineteenth century, Robert Maturin wrote *Melmoth the Wanderer*; and the Polish Jean Potocki wrote *Le Manuscript trouve a Saragosse* in French and later translated it into English under the title, *The Saragossa Manuscript*. According to Irwin, Beckford, Potocki, and Jacques Cazotte, are the founding fathers of modern fantasy literature.[56] Cazotte and the Syrian priest Dom Chavis also wrote *Suite des mille et une nuits*, which is "in part, a genuine translation of Arab tales (being based on the Paris Bibliotheque nationale MS arabe 1723)."[57] These tales were later translated into English by Robert Heron as *The Arabian Tales*. Thomas Moore published *Lalla Rookh* in 1817; Lord Byron produced his poems, "Don Juan," *The Giaour*, and *The Corsair*. More nineteenth century works such as Thomas Hope's *Anastasias*, James Morier's *Hajji Baba of Isfahan*, Alexander Kinklake's *Eothen*, William Makepeace Thackeray's *Notes of a Journey from Cornhill to Grand Cairo*, and Benjamin Disraeli's *Tancred* carry oriental characteristics connected in some way or another to *The Nights*. This world classic also affected Samuel Taylor Coleridge in "The Rime of the Ancient Mariner," "Christabel," and "Kubla Khan;" Thomas De Quincey in his memoir, *Suspiria de profundis*; Wordsworth's *The Prelude*; and Tennyson's "Recollections of the Arabian Nights." Charles Dickens's works *Christmas Carol, Hard Times*, and *The Mystery of Edwin Drood* reveal traces of the world of *The Nights*. George Meredith wrote *The Shaving of Shagpat: An Arabian Entertainment* in 1855 as a parody of *The Nights*; Robert Louis Stevenson was influenced by Meredith's book and wrote *New Arabian Nights* in 1882. Washington Irving wrote *The Conquest of Granada* and *Legends of the Alhambra*. Edgar Allan Poe was slightly affected by *The Nights* in his work *Tales of the Grotesque and Arabesque*, published in 1840. Poe was profoundly affected by *The Nights* in his famous short story "The Thousand-and-Second Tale of Scheherazade." Herman Melville's *Moby Dick* is "enriched by covert embedded references to the *Nights* and other sources of nineteenth-century culture."[58]

In the twentieth century, James Joyce's *Ulysses* (1922) has a covert affinity with Sinbad the sailor. Joyce's *Finnegans Wake* (1939), which the well-known literary critic Ihab Hassan thinks has affinities with postmodern fiction, has many allusions to *The Nights*. Marcel Proust's masterpiece *A la recherche du temps*

---

[54] Irwin *Companion* 241
[55] *Companion* 253
[56] Irwin *Companion* 260
[57] Irwin *Companion* 262
[58] *Companion* 278

perdu (Remembrance of Things Past) resembles *The Nights* in character depiction, themes, and incidents. In the Argentinean Jorge Luis Borges' works, *The Nights* is "a key text, perhaps the key text."[59] In his collections, *Labyrinth: Selected Stories and Other Writings* and *Seven Nights* there are many short stories and essays with oriental flavor such as "The Thousand and One Nights," "Averroes' Search," "Tlon, Uqbar, Orbis Tertius," "The Garden of Forking Paths," and "The Zahir." Borges' creativity and new style in writing narratives, and his long occupation with *The Nights* has led him to become one of the twentieth century's most important experimental fiction writers. In his short story, "The Garden of Forking Paths" (1941), Borges wrote of night 602, which is in the middle of *The Nights* when Shahrazad narrates the story of *The Nights*, "establishing the risk of coming once again to the night when she must repeat it, and thus on to infinity."[60] This short story is loaded with metafictional properties long before the rise and theorization of metafiction in the West. Borges was fascinated by *The Nights*, as the cultural attic of the *Nights* furnished Borges with metaphysical themes, and Borges found in the *Nights* precisely what he was hoping to find—doppelgangers, self-reflexiveness, labyrinthine structures and paradoxes, and especially paradoxes of circularity and infinity.[61]

In Egypt, several works that are built on *The Nights* or were greatly affected by it appeared before the middle of the twentieth century. *Shahrazad* is a play by Tawfiq Al-Hakim that appeared in 1934. It is about Shahrazad and Shahrayar after the end of the thousand and one nights of story-telling. Shahrayar is unhappy as he realizes that Shahrazad has been telling him stories just to save her neck; otherwise, she is not in love with him, and Shahrayar starts looking for truth and amusement through travel. It is important to note that Al-Hakim's play was translated into French in 1936 and into English in 1945, but there is no reference to it in Robert Irwin's *The Arabian Nights: A Companion*.

Al Qasr Al Mas'hoor (The Enchanted Palace) is a novel published in 1936 and co-authored by Taha Husein and Tawfiq Al Hakim, and it has the atmosphere of the great classic. *Ahlam Shahrazad (The Dreams of Shahrazad)* is a novel by Taha Husein published in 1942. It starts on the thousand and ninth night and continues until the thousand and fourteenth night. *Ahlam Shahrazad* stresses on the fact that Shahrayar misses story-telling especially at night. Shahrazad's stories of the realm of *The Nights* had ended, so Shahrayar seeks the presence of Shahrazad even while she is asleep to console himself. To his astonishment, he finds her narrating stories to him in her dreams! *Ahlam Shahrazad* reflects its author's views of the international situation of World War II, and that of Egypt on the edge of a revolution to end the monarchy.

In 1941, Suhayr al-Qalamawi's PhD dissertation on the *Nights* participated in renewing Arab interest in this classic.[62] Ferial Ghazoul says that Qalamawi's

---

[59] Irwin *Companion* 282

[60] Byatt "The Greatest Story" 169

[61] Irwin *Companion* 283

[62] "In 1935, Al-Qalamawi published a collection of short stories entitled Ahadith Jaddati (My Grandmother's Stories)... Al-Qalamawi thus used the form of *The Thousand and*

study "was a provocative project for academia, and the study proved to be a pioneering step in unleashing the critical faculties and creative powers of many writers."[63] Actually, renewed interest in *The Nights* had started a few years earlier with Tawfiq Al-Hakim's *Shahrazad*, Al-Hakim's and Taha Husein's *Al-Qasr Al Mas'hour*, and Husein's *Ahlam Shahrazad*.

In 1953, Ali Ahmad Ba-Kathir produced *Sir Shahrazad* (*The Secret of Shahrazad*), a play that reworks the whole of *The Nights* from another perspective. In Ba-Kathir's reworking of the main frame narrative of *The Nights*, Shahrayar's first wife is innocent, and Shahrayar plots her infidelity in order to kill her to cover up his own impotence. Shahrazad in this play is intelligent enough to grasp the nature of Shahrayar's dilemma and she implicitly praises Shahrayar's manhood in order to save her life. Ba-Kathir's play was also translated into French in 1954.

From the 1970s onward, studies concerning *The Nights* by Arab scholars in the Arab World or abroad, such as Ferial Ghazoul and Rasheed El-Enany, continued to enrich criticism of this classic. A few years later, the Egyptian Naguib Mahfouz and the American John Barth made use of *The Nights*; they are two influential figures in their occupation with this classic, but both will not be discussed here since a whole chapter will be devoted to each one of them. Salman Rushdie is yet another influential writer who was inspired by *The Nights*. His work *Haroun and the Sea of Stories* deals with the protagonist fighting an evil who wants to drain the sea of stories.

The Nights has been a source of inspiration throughout the ages. "Familiarity with the oriental storytelling tradition had a liberating effect on writers in the late eighteenth century, freeing them from the constraints of plausibility."[64] In the nineteenth and twentieth centuries, on the other hand, writers of fiction have used *The Nights* of the past to read and explain the present. In the twentieth century, *The Nights* has also become a bottomless source for creativity as it contains "early and exotic examples of framing, self-reference, embedded references, hidden patterns, recursion, and intertextuality."[65] These characteristics in *The Nights* are the exact characteristics of what has been theorized during the era of postmodernism as metafiction centuries after the compilation of *The Nights*.

The above brief history of *The Nights* and of the writers who made use of it to open up their fiction to limitless dimensions is necessary to be included to show the impact of this classic on world literature. In order to pay justice to The Nights and recognize it as *the* source of metafictional techniques in literature, this chapter first presents the creative plot of this masterpiece, and then explains in detail the metafictional narrative techniques in it.

The main plot of the famous story: There is an old just king who, before his death, divided his kingdom between his two sons, Shahrayar and Shahzaman.

One Nights and introduced contemporary material into it, producing a text new in both form and content" (Ashour et.al. 114).
[63] Ferial Ghazoul *Nocturnal Poetics* 135
[64] Irwin *Companion* 254
[65] Irwin *Companion* 278

The two sons, each in his own kingdom, are as just and contented as their father. Time passes by, and the eldest of the two, Shahrayar, yearns to see his brother, so he sends his wazir to the kingdom of his brother to let him know of his yearning. Shahzaman decides to travel to see his elder brother, but, after leaving his capital with his guards and loads, he remembers that he had forgotten a jewel he intends to give to his brother Shahrayar as present. Shahzaman goes back privately in the middle of the night to fetch it. When Shahzaman enters his own bed chamber, he finds his queen in the arms of a black slave in his own bed. He kills them both and leaves unnoticed and continues his trip to his brother's kingdom. While there, he becomes sick because of the agony of his wife's infidelity to the extent of not being able to accompany his brother Shahrayar on a hunting trip outside the capital. Unable to sleep, Shahzaman wanders in the middle of the night and accidentally witnesses the shocking group infidelity of his brother's queen and ten of her lady servants in the garden of the palace in the absence of Shahrayar. Seeing this, the health of Shahzaman returns to normal as he discovers that all women and not only his wife are unfaithful. Upon returning from his hunting trip, Shahrayar notices the change in his brother's health and begs him to tell about what had happened. Shahzaman tells his brother the story of what he had seen of both their wives. Together, they arranged for another hunting trip in order to come back in disguise so Shahrayar can see for himself the unfaithfulness of his queen and her lady servants. When he does, Shahrayar and his brother decide to wander the Earth to find someone with a worst calamity than theirs. While traveling, they hear stories of more unfaithful women. The response of Shahrayar is quite simple. After having become convinced that the adultery of his wife is no accident, but rather the manifestation of the true nature of women, Shahrayar considers all women unfaithful. Upon returning to his kingdom, Shahrayar decides to marry a virgin every night and slay her the next morning. This brutal act continues for about three years until no virgin is left in his kingdom but his senior wazir's daughter, Shahrazad, the learnt wise and beautiful woman. The wazir is not willing to hand his own daughter to king Shahrayar, but she convinces her father to do so telling him that she has a plan to stop these killings.

The Nights, the huge fictional construct strongly displays clear characteristics of metafiction that appear in the overall structure of *The Nights*, in its creative presentation of reality and unreality, and in other metafictional techniques that give *The Nights* its distinctive flavor. *The Nights'* complex overall framing structure continues to dazzle readers as well as professional authors of fiction over the ages. The first frame-story of Kings Shahrayar and Shahzaman, even before Shahrazad enters the narrative scene with her ocean of stories within stories, is the first framing device that depends on story-telling of narratives of the infidelities of the two queens, and the two kings' search for other narratives of female infidelity to prove to themselves that all women are unfaithful. The second framing device in *The Nights* includes Shahrazad's stories within stories. Patricia Waugh, in her book *Metafiction*, refers to the narrative frame of stories within stories as "Chinese-box structures which contest the reality of each individual 'box' through a nesting of narrators."[66] The third framing device in *The Nights* is the division into nights which is an exclusive characteristic of this great classic as Richard Burton says, "without the nights, no *Arabian Nights*."[67] These narrative frames magnify the metafictional elements in *The Nights* as frames "are essential in all fiction. They become more perceptible as one moves from realist to modernist modes and are explicitly laid bare in metafiction."[68] There are other perceptible small-scale frames in *The Nights*. Whenever there is a story that encompasses other stories, the main story serves as a frame for stories and tales within it. For example, "The Story of the Porter and the Three Ladies" serves as a frame for the tales within it, one of which is "The Second Dervish's Tale." This tale is also a frame for a tale within it, which is "The Tale of the Envious and the Envied." All the above frames in *The Nights* are essential components to the structure of this world classic. Waugh's recognition of framing as a device associated more with metafiction dissociates the start of metafiction from the postmodern era and takes it far back to *The Nights* even though Waugh does not mention *The Nights* as a literary text dependent on framing and frames.

The framing structure of *The Nights*, takes a fascinating step with the character Shahrazad. From her first night as bride, it was up to her, with the help of her sister Dunyazad, to carry on the art of story-telling and fill a thousand and one nights with a continuous flow of narration of fiction. Shahrazad here is an idealized character that is able through a defined narrative plan of the second framing device to overcome in size and importance the first frame narrative of the ordeal of Shahrayar. Although the second framing device of Shahrazad telling stories within stories for many nights stems from Shahrayar's story or the first framing device, it (Shahrazad's frame of narratives) is far more memorable and important than the first framing device, creating a narcissistic text and a neurotic narrative.

It is important to note that neither Grant Stirling, in his long and important article "Neurotic Narrative: Metafiction and Object-Relation Theory," who discusses the relationship between neurotic narratives and metafiction in light of object-relation theory; nor Linda Hutcheon in her informative book *Narcissistic Narrative* mention *The Nights* and/or its structure as suitable candidates for analysis using object-relation theory. The following examination proposes *The Nights*' suitability to be analyzed as a metafictional neurotic narrative using methodology from Stirling's article and Hutcheon's book.

The story of King Shahrayar as an aggressive character who represents threat of death to all young women occupies a small space in the overall space of *The Nights* when compared to the huge space that the stories of Shahrazad occupy. Also, the stories that Shahrazad narrates underestimates, in some way or another, Shahrayar's ordeal to the extent of curing him of his obsession to kill women. For a period of about three years, Shahrazad narrates stories to capture his

---

[66] Waugh 30
[67] Richard Burton xxxi
[68] Waugh 30

attention and force him to refrain from ordering her execution only to hear the conclusion of a story that she postpones to the following night. The characters of Shahrazad, Shahrayar, and their narrative setting explained above are examples of metafictional narrative narcissism known in object-relation theory. Shahrayar is the subject, and Shahrazad is his significant object as the elements of aggression and idealization that define narcissism in object-relations theory can be transposed into a critical typology that concisely expresses the primary narrative impulses that metafictional texts tend to erect within their own narrative matrices.[69]

Within the narrative matrix of *The Nights*, narcissistic narrative "transforms the authorial process of shaping, of making, into part of the pleasure and challenge of reading as a co-operative, interpretive experience."[70] Because of this (and other) overt narrative/metafictional techniques in *The Nights*, reading this classic has been creating an inexhaustible pleasure not only for the common reader but also for professional writers of fiction as well.

Also, the created tension where Shahrazad is in a state of defense is psychoanalytically "expressed through libidinal cathexis"[71] characteristic of metafictional narcissistic narratives. The depiction of the character Shahrazad as defensive in the face of the threat of death creates a marvelous setting for a continued concentration of emotional energy on story-telling that lasts for approximately a thousand nights. This marvelous setting of Shahrazad's emotional energy represents an ideal situation of narcissistic narratives in *The Nights*.

In the second frame of *The Nights* where Shahrazad is the narrator, the structure of plots is built on story-telling. The powerful cruel Shahrayar becomes a passive narratee (functioning as a reader) in front of Shahrazad's stories. Shahrayar's passivity continues as his narrator, Shahrazad, tells him stories within stories with other embedded narratives and different narrators speaking through her. These embedded narratives work as interruption devices to hold the interest of Shahrayar and take his mind away from his reality with Shahrazad to the irrealities of her stories. Interruption is a well-known device in metafiction.

The third framing device of the division into nights presents another narrative/metafictional characteristic where stories or tales are interrupted with the first light of day. At the approaching dawn of each night of *The Nights*, the following statement (or something similar depending on the translation) goes,

"But dawn broke and morning overtook Shahrazad and she lapsed into silence. Then Dunyazad said, 'sister, what a lovely story!' Shahrazad replied, 'what is this compared with what I shall tell you tomorrow night? It will be even better; it will be more wonderful, delightful, entertaining, and delectable if the King spares me and lets me live.'"

This or similar statements that divide this work into nights serve as patterns of interruption making a classical distinction between the fictional world of

---

[69] Stirling "Neurotic Narrative" 82
[70] Hutcheon *Narcissistic Narrative* 154
[71] Stirling "NeuroticNarrative" 82

Shahrazad's stories and the supposedly nonfictional world of her story with Shahrayar. Richard Van Leeuwen, in his article, "The Art of Interruption: *The Thousand and One Nights* and Jan Potocki" published in 2004, recognizes some of the affinities between *The Nights* and metafiction. Leeuwen says, "The division of *The Nights* into nights creates a form of interruption…a form of breaking something whole, which seems to challenge the continuation of the narrative and the unity of the work."[72] "In fact," Leeuwen adds, "the whole text of *The Thousand and One Nights* is nothing more than the account of an interruption, a long dialogic confrontation with the readers."[73] This metafictional characteristic of interruption is discussed by Waugh who says:

"Any text that draws the reader's attention to its process of construction by frustrating his or her conventional expectations of meaning and closure problematizes more or less explicitly the ways in which narrative codes— whether 'literary' or 'social'— artificially construct apparently 'real' and imaginary worlds in the terms of particular ideologies while presenting these as transparently 'natural' and 'eternal.'"[74]

In addition, the division into nights serves a dual purpose, in the opinion of Haddawy. First, it keeps Shahryar and the reader waiting for actions to be continued the following night. Second, it enables the reader to realize a division between the fictional world of the stories and tales and the realistic world of Shahrayar and Shahrazad.[75] In other words, it enables the reader to be involved in a multi-layered fictional world of aesthetic pleasure.

Moreover, the framing device of the division into nights points to another metafictional property of binary oppositions. It points not only to night/day and dark/light but also to the "seen and the unseen, clarity and mystery, openness and closeness, the rational and the irrational, purity and sin, control and chaos"[76] associated with the inherited difference between day and night. *The Nights*, therefore, contains binary oppositions acknowledge by Leeuwen not as binary oppositions but as "interruptions [that serve] as a structural device linked to temporal divisions."[77] These interruptions allow Shahrazad to juxtapose Shahriyar's world with another reality, the reality of fantasy and the imagination, carefully structured to instruct and to convey a message. The two worlds are separated by a regular interruption, the appearance of daylight, but Shahrazad convinces Shahriyar that her stories have a bearing upon life in daytime, that the two realms are separated but linked to each other. She restores the duality in Shahriyar's personality, while at the same time bringing the two components in harmony and establishing a new form of continuity.[78]

---

72 Richard Van Leeuwen 183

73 Leeuwen 191

74 Waugh 22

75 Haddawy xiii

76 Leeuwen 92

77Leeuwen 94

78 Leeuwen 93

The binary oppositions of day and night, therefore, is a narrative device of structure that highlights the relationship between day as a time for serious real life and night as time fit for leisure and narrative, which here represents a form of play.

Furthermore, *The Nights* framing structure of the division into nights can be seen, in light of object-relation theory, as a splitting device used to split stories, which are usually whole-objects, into part-objects divided by time. The character Shahrazad operates as the psychoanalytical device of idealizing transference which "serves the narcissistic needs of the analysand by saving a part of the lost experience of primary narcissism assigning it to an archaic, rudimentary (transitional) self-object [the analyst]."[79] Shahrazad is the analyst "experienced as an extension of the archaic grandiose self"[80] attained by her role as story-teller. The character Shahrayar is an analysand in need for completion of a story or tale which is postponed to the following night. The existence of this type of transference is, according to Stirling, "one of the best and most reliable diagnostic signs of narcissism"[81] used to analyze metafictional texts. This situation becomes a critical typology in which the transferential models usefully illuminate how metafictional texts thematize the activity of reading whereas the process of splitting addresses the fragmentation of plot so commonly found in metafictional texts.[82]

Between the two characters, splitting into nights becomes, therefore, a form of fragmentation that contributes to the overall matrix of *The Nights*. Kenneth Millard deals with the metafictional characteristic of fragmentation, in the novel *High Lonesome* in his article, "The Metafictional Aesthetic of *High Lonesome*," but his analysis can be applied to fragmentation in *The Nights*. Millard says that fragmentation is prompted as redemptive and transformative in a cultural setting in which the question of artistic value is in a state of crisis, where the artist must strive to examine what is worthy and honorable in art as a necessary and integral part of any creative enterprise worth prosecuting.[83]

The artist and fictional character Shahrazad of *The Nights* is in a state of crisis as she fragments her stories in order to redeem herself and transform her situation.

Within the framing structures of *The Nights*, Shahrazad is self-conscious of the act of story-telling, and Shahrayar is also self-conscious of the fictional nature of the stories that Shahrazad is narrating. Also, the reader of *The Nights* is well aware of at least the fictionality of the stories Shahrazad is narrating as he is constantly reminded each and every end of night of that fictionality. *The Nights*, therefore, is "fictional writing which self-consciously and systematically

---

[79] Stirling "Neurotic Narrative" 84
[80] Stirling "Neurotic Narrative" 84
[81] Stirling "Neurotic Narrative" 84
[82] Stirling "Neurotic Narrative" 85
[83] Kenneth Millard 252

draws attention to its status as an artifact…"[84] This great classic, therefore, meets the most widely accepted definition of metafiction.

From another perspective, it is well-known that *The Nights* has been structured over hundreds of years by unknown author/authors. The absence of a known author gives *The Nights* a unique position of a relationship between this whole text and its readers. This can be observed when looking at the numerous translations of *The Nights* that rely on different available texts of *The Nights* and the differences in these texts and translations in terms of number of stories, deviations from original texts and sources, and amount of information or details each and every one of these translations has. In addition, intentions and purposes of each translator of *The Nights* create new texts with contexts that fall under the umbrella of the original. "The history of the *Nights* offers the amusing and unique picture of a text writing its authors, who in turn remake it in their own images."[85] The reader, therefore, is faced with a text that has become, over time and numerous versions, a kind of strange magical entity. This entity is attained by the fact that "All texts are altered by a change in how they are perceived. All selves and cultures are also altered by a change in how they are perceived."[86] This unique position of *The Nights* is highly metafictional where texts are praised for their flexibility and magical properties.[87]

It is also accepted that many of the stories within *The Nights* are well known folk tales from the folklore of numerous civilizations. Some of them are parts of known fictional works like *Kalila wa Dimna* as most of the animal stories. Others are ancient tales such as "'The Adventures of Bulukiyya' (which is the tale of the quest of a pre-Islamic king for immortality) from *the Epic of Gilgamesh.*"[88] Shahrazad, the narrator, is not inventing the tales she is narrating or imitating the real world of fiction; she is retelling already known and loved tales. *The Nights,* therefore, meets John Barth's definition of metafiction as it is "a novel [work of fiction] that imitates a novel [already known units of fiction] rather than the real world."

In addition, the narration or inclusion of already well known and appreciated tales within the structure of *The Nights* displays reflexivity and intertextuality, which represent other characteristics of metafiction. Shahrazad's stories are reflexive of folk tales in other fictional structures known within the culture, and texts within texts in *The Nights* represent intertextuality full scale. Brenda K. Marshall comments on this by saying:

"Intertextuality is precisely a momentary compendium of everything that has come before and is now. Intertextuality calls attention to prior texts in the sense that it acknowledges that no text can have meaning without those prior texts, it is a space where 'meanings' intersect."[89]

---

[84] Waugh 2

[85] Sallis 84

[86] Sallis 84

[87] See Ghazoul's *Nocturnal Poetics* for more on *The Nights* as a multiplicity of texts.

[88] Irwin *Companion* 74

[89] Brenda K. Marshall 128

With its wealth of stories and tales from different historical periods, *The Nights* is a rich metafictional body of meaningful collective experiences.

Moreover, to broaden the scope of literary studies, the celebration of textuality in fiction and viewing a fictional work as text is a phenomenon that has fascinated critics of literature from the 1960s, the time of the rise of metafictional experimentation, and on. Metafiction, which involves criticism of literary texts and literary texts themselves, has prompted critics to look not for unity in a work of art but to look for textuality. Instead of works with beginnings, bodies, and ends, critics have been attracted to works which were 'pastiches' of other works that added up to the meaning obtained from the overall texts. *The Nights* is a pastiche of many many works that contribute not only depth and variety but also meaning to literary studies of this classic.

Furthermore, even though *The Nights* has become available to Western readers through French and English translations during the realist period when artificiality of fiction was concealed and works of fiction were structured to resemble the real world, it is obvious that the very structure of *The Nights* celebrates its artificiality. This celebration of artificiality appears in the exaggeration of the complexity of the narrative construct of stories within stories within stories. The stories "The Hunchback" and "The Porter and the Three Ladies" are excellent examples of stories that embody other different stories narrated by different characters in an artificial and complicated construct that celebrates artificiality. This narrative quality of artificiality was probably most appealing to Western readers when *The Nights* became available through translation in the beginning of the eighteenth century. This artificiality is metafictional as Metafiction "is an art that recognizes its own artificiality, its own systematic existence."[90] In *The Nights*, there is "world within world: the concept of irreality"[91] that is not ashamed of fictionality.

The irreality in *The Nights* provides the reader with worlds of aesthetic pleasure "derived from the escape into an exotic world of wish fulfillment and from the underlying act of transformation and the consequent pleasure, which may be best defined in Freudian terms as the sudden overcoming of an obstacle."[92] Through this angle, *The Nights* is an artificial metafictional text as metafiction offers extremely accurate models for understanding the contemporary experience of the world as a construct, an artifice, a web of interdependent semiotic systems, readers of metafiction are invited, though not compelled, to question how their own worlds are similar textually.[93]

The artificiality of story-telling in the structure of *The Nights* appears over and over again with Shahrazad's intrusion to cut the flow of narration each night. Her act is an unusual violation of common narrative levels as she herself is a fictional character. On each and every night, Shahrazad intrudes into the narration process by reminding Shahrayar that she is a narrator telling him stories

---

[90] Davidson 484
[91] Page Stranahan Elrod 11
[92] Haddawy xiii
[93] Stirling "Neurotic Narrative" 81–82

that were once told to her. At the beginning of each and every night Shahrazad self-consciously addresses the device of fiction and starts her narration (which might be slightly different according to different versions of *The Nights*) by saying, "It is related, O wise and Happy King that…" At the end of each night with the break of dawn, the extradiegetic narrator, not Shahrazad, steps in and again self-consciously and directly addresses the device of fiction by saying, "But morning overtook Shahrazad, and she lapsed into silence." On some nights, Shahrazad's sister Dunyazad says, "What a strange and wonderful story!" Shahrazad, then, replies, "Tomorrow night I shall tell something even stranger and more wonderful than this." These textual units are given significance beyond language's signifying capacity. They have power that stops the flow of fiction; power that exceeds that of King Shahrayar himself. These words are forms of 'Direct Address' that bring the reader, through the listeners Shahrayar and Dunyazad, to dramatic points that highlight the aesthetic value of story-telling as savior of the life of Shahrazad. These textual units serve as reminders that the extradiegetic narrator and Shahrazad, the intradiegetic narrator, have to suspend telling stories. This suspension of narration is a metafictional characteristic where "suspending the narration to create the effect of immediacy is inextricably bound with oral situations. Metafiction draws on…features of Direct Address (DA) in order to promote the reader's involvement. The reader is invited into the text."[94] Georgakopoulou, who does not refer to *The Nights* as having this direct address quality in her article "Discursive Aspects of Metafiction: A Neo-Oral Aura?" refers to this narrator interaction within a text as 'metacommunication.' In metafiction, metacommunication, Georgakopoulou believes, "is a particularly powerful component of the narrative. The narrators constantly foreground the text's discursive situation. Their interest in the dynamics of the text's interactive powers shapes their stance."[95]

In *The Nights*, direct address is apparent in Shahrazad's role as a character playing games on her audience, her king, and us readers, and structuring her world of fiction around the notion of narrating stories. She represents here the authorial presence even though we, readers, do realize that she herself is a character in the work in our hands. "This self-conscious awareness of the authorial presence in the work corresponds also to the…emphasis on self-reflexivity and metafiction."[96] This awareness is acknowledged by Waugh who says:

"The more a text insists on its linguistic condition, the further it is removed from the everyday context of 'common sense' invoked by realistic fiction. Metafictional texts show that literary fiction can never imitate or 'represent' the world but always imitates or 'represents' the discourses which in turn construct that world."[97]

---

[94] Alexandra Georgakopoulou 3
[95] Georgakopoulou 3
[96] Elrod 10
[97] Waugh 100

Even though it was immensely popular when it was translated into Western languages, *The Nights* has not been incorporated into literary theory probably for two reasons. First, *The Nights* is not part of the Western literary canon.[98] Second, *The Nights* is a text that insists on its linguistic condition. Borges in his article "Partial Magic in the Quixote" considers the linguistic consciousness of narration in *The Nights* a clear example of an artificially constructed world where a narrator is inverted or embedded into another fictional construct. Borges says, "these inversions suggest that if the characters of a fictional work can be readers or spectators [as is the case of Shahrayar], we, its readers or spectators, can be fictitious."[99] This idea of the possibility of the fictionality of the so-called 'real' world is one of the forces that pushed authors of fiction during the 1960s and 70s to look for fictional strategies that reflect the ambiguity of what is real and what is not real in contemporary life.

In the formal structure of *The Nights*, storytelling as an artifice is explicitly foregrounded within the narrative not only in the repetition of phrases at each dawn but also in embedding stories or narratives within narratives. In other words, there is a complex use of embedded narratives where there is a presence of more than one narrator and narratee. Although Shahrazad is an influential character, she is not the sole narrator of *The Nights*. While she is an active intradiegetic narrator, she is introduced into the narrative of Shahrayar by an unnamed extradiegetic narrator. What is unique in *The Nights* is that Shahrazad is not only narrating her own experiences but stories of others while actively being part of the overall narrative of *The Nights*, making her also a homodiegetic narrator. Her narratives represent a complex intricate web of texts drawn from already known human folklore, making these narratives of alternative realities universal meta texts. Before she becomes the main narrator of stories to Shahrayar, Shahrazad has to listen to stories narrated by her father, the grand wazir who tries to convince her, his daughter, of not scarifying herself to Shahrayar by telling her the fairytale stories of "The Ox and the Donkey" and "The Merchant and His Wife." She becomes a narratee listening and commenting on the stories of her father who becomes another homodiegetic narrator. This foregrounding of the intricate webs of story-telling in *The Nights* is metafictional as there are deconstructions of the usual realist concepts of story-telling. The extradiegetic narrator is pushed aside and the intradiegetic narrators (the wazir narrating the two stories, and Shahrazad narrating hundreds of stories within stories), who are also homodiegetic narrators, are foregrounded. This intricate relationship of narration is a characteristic of metafictional texts.

Also, including stories of conversing animals and bringing unusual human properties such as understanding animal tongs as in "The tale of the Ox and the Donkey" further deconstruct the usual modernist modes of narratives in terms of relating the story of the ox and the donkey and that of the merchant and his wife to Shahrazad's situation. Ironically, Shahrazad does not take her father's advice into consideration and goes on with her decision to marry Shahrayar as she is not

---

[98] See above, p. 15
[99] Borges Labyrinths 196

dumb like the donkey or stupid like the merchant's wife. The juxtaposition of all of this in the first frame of *The Nights* does not produce chaos; on the contrary, everything there is highly defined by the roles the extradiegetic, intradiegetic, and homodiegetic narrators play. This insistence on story-telling takes the text of *The Nights* right into the realm of metafiction.

Another metafictional characteristic in the structure of *The Nights* is that it is open-ended on the level of each story or tale and its capacity to add more tales on the level of the work as a whole. On the level of each story or tale, the beginning or resuming of narration is highlighted and marked, from one perspective, with Shahrazad being alive for another night only to complete telling a story. Instead of ending her stories with the coming of dawn, Shahrazad, the narrator, keeps Shahrayar and the reader in the pure pleasure of anticipation of the beginning of the following night. From another perspective, stories in *The Nights* vary in length and complexity. They range from rudimentary, eroded, or fragmented sketches which recall the general features of the summary of a proto-text given by Ibn al-Nadim in the 10th/4th centuries to literary, crafted versions which appear in MSS of the 16th/10th, 17th/11th and 19th/13th centuries.[100]

The need for a closer, argues Sallis, is a product of the growing awareness of the short story as a genre that requires completeness in the form of a closer[101]. The original *Nights* with its fragmented nature and open-ended stories or tales, therefore, is more attached to metafiction than the refined later translations of The Nights such as Galland's, Payne's, and Burton's.

On the level of the book as a whole, *The Nights'* open flexible structure allows for adding more narratives under the umbrella of the main outer frame narrative without seriously affecting the overall meaning of the work. This is why there are numerous equally enjoyable versions of *The Nights* ranging from 16 volumes, in the case of Burton's translation, to a slender volume, such as Haddawy's translation. Also, on the level of the book as a whole, this flexible structure allows for differences between versions in their content of stories; the best example of which is the stories: "Aladdin and the Magic Lamp," "Ali Baba and the Forty Thieves," and "Sinbad the Sailor" which appear in Galland version but not in the supposedly 14th century original version.

In addition, the open-enddeness of *The Nights* has been a source of inspiration and a dazzling construct for major inventive fiction writers throughout the ages. Driven by that open-enddeness to the degree of including modern science discoveries of the eighteenth century, Edgar Allan Poe wrote his short story, "The Thousand-and-second Tale of Scheherazade." In this story, King Shahrayar kills Shahrazad after the thousand and second night because he did not believe the inventions (Poe meant the discoveries of science of the period) she tells him about in her tale of the adventure of Sinbad the sailor.

Jorge Luis Borges was also inspired by the open-enddeness of *The Nights* and worked to make use, in the world of fiction, of its vast possibilities of invention. First of all, "Borges loved the open-enddeness of the title 'The

---

[100] Sallis 97
[101] Sallis 97

Thousand and One Nights,' that is, a thousand, standing for infinity, having still one night added to it, and play with this openness."[102] Borges also exploited the roles of allusion to *The Nights* seeking unlimited interpretations. In Borges book *Seven Nights*, he insists that there is no need to read this huge work as it lives in the consciousness of each and every one of us. In his story about the magic night 602, a story not in any version of *The Nights* but in his imagination, Borges lets Shahrazad narrate her own story to Shahrayar which means re-telling all stories and tales in *The Nights* indefinitely. Borges also stresses on the open-endedness of *The Nights* with his book, *The Book of Sands*, where "neither sand nor this book has a beginning or an end."[103] The flexibility of *The Nights* makes *The Book of Sands* "a book that is only an incipit a book with no ending."[104]

The Nights presents yet another metafictional property of structure. In this timeless literary work, there is a mixture between literary genres. *The Nights* can be viewed as a novel; this novel contains numerous recognizable short stories of various complexity and length. *The Nights* also incorporates poetry inside its prose structure. In its space, *The Nights* literary genres intersect and neutralize one another, creating a metafictional literary text.

To conclude the discussion of the affinity between the structure of *The Nights* and metafiction, it is appropriate to include the words of John Barth, the metafictionist most occupied with *The Nights*,

"Closer inspection reveals that the real 'frame' of *the 1001 Nights* is not the relation between Scheherazade and Shahryar, but something 'farther out' and more ancient: the relation between the reader, or listener, and the unspecified teller of the story of Scheherazade. I mean this literally: The opening words of the tale (after the invocation to Allah) are "there is a book called *the 1001 Nights*, in which it is said that once upon a time…" etc. In other words, *the 1001 Nights* is not immediately about Scheherazade and her stories; it is about a book called *the 1001 Nights*, which *is* about Scheherazade and her stories."[105]

Barth therefore is acknowledging that the whole structure of this great classic is a main component of the book that is generating interest over the ages. *The Nights'* highly intricate structure that looks chaotic while it is not requires further recognition, importance, and affinity with metafiction with the spread of the applications of notions of chaos theory in fiction.

Chaos theory[106] as a science started accidently in the early 1960s when Edward Lorenz, a weather specialist, was using a simple digital computer to input his weather predictions. One day, he came back to check his data and instead of entering all six digits, he only entered the first three digits thinking the last three will not make much difference. He was surprised to see that the data of the predictions that appeared on the screen were different from the ones he saw

---

[102] Fishburn 213

[103] Fishburn 216

[104] Byatt xix

[105] Barth *Friday Book* 223

[106] "Chaos does not, despite the common sense of the word, mean randomness, but nonlinearity; it does lack predictability, but it has discernible form" (Polvinen 7).

in his first predictions. He concluded that small changes at the beginning of a complex dynamical system (any type of system) could lead to long-term large changes. He also concluded that in any dynamical system there is order underlaying chaos. Lorenz's ideas developed into new mathematical formulae known as chaos theory that spread from the fields of science into other fields of study including the humanities. Chaos theory, which is also known as complexity theory, non-linear dynamics, and chaology, is being assimilated into literature and literary studies from the 1980s as "at least some Postmodernist writers and critics may find in chaology a ground metaphor…as suggestive for them [writers] as 'Persian' carpet design and 'Eastern' frame-tale collections were for Schlegel and his comrades."[107]

It appears, therefore, that *The Nights*, with its complex non-linear, intricate, and dynamical structure that looks chaotic but is highly organized, provides a form of invitation for critics to analyze it using chaos theory. Also, it is well-known that the scene of *The Nights* takes a new turn when Shahrazad, with her sea of stories, enters its narrative scene creating a drastic change that takes the whole work into new dimensions. Shahrazad entering the narrative scene forms the initial condition that greatly affects the narrative path of *The Nights*, and sensitivity to initial conditions is a characteristic of chaotic systems. Shahrazad's initial condition of cycles within cycles of story-telling is a structural form of creative chaos of metafiction that calls for generating further interest in this classic.

In addition to structure, *The Nights* has another perplexing metafictional characteristic, which is what Evelyn Fishburn refers to as "the relationship of life and fiction."[108] This relationship has been apparent in *The Nights* to prominent fiction writers as soon as this fiction classic reached the West.[109] Edgar Allan Poe in his short story "The Thousand and Second Tale of Scheherazade" (published in 1845) starts with a statement: "Truth is stranger than fiction." Poe was probably influenced by the words of Richard Burton, the famous translator of *The Nights* into English. In his spectacular preface to his translation, Burton offers thorough explanations of his translation of *The Nights* as a marvelous literary text, and of the reflections of Arab and Moslem life the Western reader could learn from reading *The Nights* through his translation. Burton says that readers "will readily and pleasantly learn more of the Moslem's manners and customs, laws and religion than is known to the average Orientalist."[110] Burton also says in the same preface, "These volumes [*The Nights*], moreover, offered me a long-sought opportunity of noticing practices and customs which interest all mankind."[111] In addition, Burton not only tries to preserve, in his translation,

---

[107] Barth *Further Fridays* 328
[108] Evelyn Fishburn 213
[109] Ghazoul says the roots of *The Nights* are in The Panchatantra which is essentially a political manual handed down in the form of a narrative work (Nocturnal Poetics 135).
[110] Burton xi
[111] Burton xxxvi

the facts of life and living, but he tries to keep intact the linguistic and fictional context of this massive work as he says:

"My work claims to be a faithful copy of the great Eastern Saga-book, by preserving intact, not only the spirit, but even the *mecanique* [sic], the manner and the matter. Hence, however prosy and long-drawn out be the formula, it retains the scheme of *The Nights* because they are a prime feature in the original."[112]

Burton's concerns of capturing the creativity in the context of *The Nights* reveal the difficult task of finding hard-to-define boundaries, highly highlighted in the debate of metafiction, between what is particular and what is universal, what is fiction and what is real in fiction. Patricia Waugh in her book *Metafiction* explains that "the ontological status of fictional objects is determined by the fact that they exist by virtue of, whilst also forming, the fictional context which is finally the words on the page."[113] Waugh adds that Metafiction "draws attention to what I shall call the *creation/description* paradox which defines the status of *all* fiction."[114] This paradox of creation can be seen in the second frame story in *The Nights*, the story of Shahrazad and Shahrayar, which forms the real world for the reader while the worlds of the tales told by Shahrazad are the unreal worlds of fiction. This variation between what is real and what is fictitious highlights the flow between real action and story action, and real violence and told violence. It ends up being a story about what story could do for a story, where the layers of story refer to complex ways to their established real world, and to the relatively unreal world of the reader.[115]

The creation of worlds in fiction paradoxically becomes alternative for the world of reality. "When life became threatening, Borges 'opened the volume of *The Arabian Nights* as though to block out reality.' The magic of fiction, therefore, becomes an alternative to reality, a means of escape from its horror and a strategy for survival."[116] Patricia Waugh discusses the metafictional characteristic of reality vs. fiction by saying:

"Although literary fiction is only a verbal reality, it constructs through language an imaginative world that has, within its own terms, full referential status as an alternative to the world in which we live… Metafiction lays bare the linguistic basis of the 'alternative worlds' constructed in literary fiction."[117]

Burton, Poe, Borges, Barth, and many other fictionists throughout the ages have recognized in *The Nights* a narrative quality which could be called now a metafictional characteristic long before metafiction has been theorized. These authors acknowledged what Waugh refers to as "the primary reality of the…linguistic context of the literary text."[118] In *The Nights*, each story can

---

[112] Burton (xxxi)
[113] Waugh 88
[114] Waugh 88
[115] Sallis 99
[116] Fishburn 217
[117] Waugh 100
[118] Waugh 87

intervene in real life; it can save or kill the prince or the reader. The climax gives all stories of the cycle their final significance. The aim is to disclose the truth, to unravel reality on the basis of allegories that, by showing its underlying 'unreal' truth, will in the end influence reality.[119]

Shahrazad, the main presenter of *The Nights*, highlights her supposedly real situation of being threatened with death with fiction.

Moreover, the creator or presenter of a fictional text, be it a direct speaking author or a character addressing the reader (as in many cases in *The Nights*), is more responsible and more involved in constructing a fictional world that could add meaning to the actual world as the new type of reader and reading that metafiction encourages can be related to ideological considerations. This means that it would be expected and/or desired that the reader's re-examining and re-evaluating of her relationship to the text and its addressee will lead her to re-examine and re-evaluate her relationship to the cultural codes and systems of the world outside it.[120]

And indeed, the notions of reality vs. fiction in *The Nights* have been gaining popularity with the passage of time as tools to explain the reality of contemporary woman in particular.

In general, the recognition of the importance of the reality/fictionality of a linguistic text took some time to be developed and theorized. During the 1960s and the 1970s, experimentation in writing fiction flourished tremendously during what is referred to as the postmodern era. Life after the two World Wars, the Cold War, and the turmoil of the 1960s, was more complicated than to be presented by the modern fiction of realism. Fiction writers, during that era, were experimenting in search of other ways to reflect life complexities. Some of them, like Thomas Pynchon in *V.*, Gilbert Sorrentino in *Crystal Vision*, John Barth in *Lost in the Funhouse*, William Gass in *Willie Master's Lonesome Wife*, Donald Barthleme in *Snow White*, and Robert Coover in *Pricksongs and Descants* did so by using totally new linguistic narrative techniques that break with previously acknowledged conventions of realism in writing fiction. Others, like Jorge Luis Borges in his short stories such as 'The Mirror of Ink, 'The Chamber of Statues,' and 'Tale of the Two Dreamers,' John Barth in *The Last Voyage of Somebody the Sailor*, Salman Rushdie in *Satanic Verses* turned to grand narratives (fiction or nonfiction) such as *The Nights* in search of fiction that reflects the surreality of life. All of these works, plus many others which are exploring the relationship of life and fiction, came to be theorized, in some way or another, as metafictional and postmodern without distinguishing between what show totally new and inventive narrative techniques and what are revivals of already existing texts. By keeping Shahrayar self-consciously aware of the fictionality of her stories, Shahrazad within the overall fictitious work, *The Nights*, linguistically continues to draw the attention of her king to the status of her stories as fiction. Here, *The Nights* stresses Borges's belief that "literature does not reflect reality but is something added to the world: not a mirror of the world, but just another thing

---

[119] Leeuwen 88
[120] Georgakopoulou 9

added to the world's content."[121] The purpose behind story-telling in *The Nights* is to change the nature of Shahrayar and his vision of justice.

From another perspective, Shahrazad the character, threatened with death if she fails to keep up the flow of fiction, has moved to be close-to-real within the overall frame of *The Nights* for readers of fiction! Yet, the context of the narrative setting of Shahrazad and her story with Shahrayar within *The Nights* is, as everyone recognizes, fictional or rather metafictional. In metafiction, "the reader is never required systematically to connect the artifice of the narrative with the problematic 'real' world, or to explore the mode of fictional presentation."[122] Narrative settings in *The Nights*, therefore, create unstable metafictional worlds where boundaries between reality and fiction seem magical.

To conclude the discussion of fictionality/reality in *The Nights*, it is important to mention that the stories and tales of this excellent work of art have dazzled readers and critics to the extent of moving them from the realm of fiction to the realm of reality or vice versa.

The tales themselves are masterpieces of the art of story-telling. In inventiveness and sheer entertainment value they stand supreme among the short stories of all times. And in their minute accuracy of detail and the vast range and variety of their subject-matter they constitute the most comprehensive and intimate record of medieval Islam. For despite the fabulous and fantastic world they portray, with its emphasis on the marvelous and the supernatural, they are a faithful mirror of the life and manners of the age which engendered them.[123]

The best example of this is the stories in the Sinbad cycle which are loaded with information about sailing and about 'every sea upon which the sun shines.' The information is so close to reality to the extent that the Khalifah Haroun Al Rasheed ordered to keep a copy of them in the archive in Baghdad as references on travel. The stories of *The Nights*' fine artistic value and the abundance of details of Muslims' life and living during a certain period of history, therefore, contribute to *The Nights*' reflection of both fact and fiction; a quality that writers of metafiction strive for as the boundaries of what is real and what is otherwise are constantly being questioned.

In addition to the metafictional characteristics in the structure of *The Nights* and its metafictional presentation of the blurring lines of reality and unreality, this massive narrative work contains other strongly recognized metafictional techniques such as its use of irony, its apparent fictionality, its universality (it even includes not only the human world but also the animal, the jinn, and supernatural worlds), and it does not separate between high and low. Irony is a literary device that brings depth to a text and establishes a relationship between reader and text. Irony is abundantly present in *The Nights*. Roy Mottahedeh, in his article "Ajai'b in *The Thousand and One Nights*," discusses several types of irony. An example is the story of "The Porter and the Three Ladies of Baghdad" where each character from Haroun al Rasheed, Ja'far the Barmecide, the three

---

[121] Fishburn 217

[122] Waugh 43

[123] N J Dawood 7

one-eyed dervishes, the porter, and the three ladies themselves has a story that other characters are not aware of until the turn of each one of them arrives to tell his or her story. This kind of irony is different from Metafictional irony in *The Nights* that appears and reappears at each night of the thousand and one nights at the approach of dawn when the character-narrator Shahrazad assumes her position as story-teller and distances herself from her fiction by interrupting her narration in order to remind Shahrayar, and the reader, that what she is narrating is not real but a work of fiction. Metafictional irony, therefore, is "a means to distance oneself from oneself."[124] When Shahrazad cuts the flow of narration, "*The Nights* enters into collusion with the reader in the construction of a system of what we might call suspense: if something astonishing is produced and something more astonishing promised, there is interest and, consequently, hope."[125] This continuous repetition of suspension is foregrounded in *The Nights* so vividly that it is hard to ignore its metafictional irony even though *The Nights* has been an enjoyable literary work for more than a thousand years before metafiction was theorized as such.

The apparent ironic metafictionality of *The Nights* coincides with similarly apparent fictionality of this great book. The fictionality of *The Nights* has amazed writers and readers as well. The narrator Shahrazad has never claimed truth of her tales. She would start a tale by saying "I heard, O happy King, that..." Or, she would finish a tale and resume the narration of the next one by saying, "O King! This is not more wondrous than the story of..." Shahrazad's sister, Dunyazad, comments on what is told by saying, for instance, "Sister, what a lovely story!" Shahrazad replies, "Tomorrow night I shall tell you something even lovelier, strange, and more wonderful if I live, the Almighty God willing." This linguistic highlighting of stories and story-telling drives the attention of the reader away from reality and toward the irreality of the text. Also, in addition to creating the possibility of multiple meanings, which in itself is a metafictional property, the embedded stories within stories in *The Nights* create a hierarchy of narrative levels, where the story of King Shahrayar's intention to kill young brides is the main or center narrative. If this main story is fictional, all other stories in *The Nights* are fictional as well. This linguistic and structural insistence on story-telling adds to the metafictionality of *The Nights*.

Shahrazad's stories are also full of ordinary human characters with common needs and earthly emotions as well as non-human characters; conversing animals, flying creatures, and immortal jinns who are capable of breaking the rules of time and space that human beings are tied to. In "The Story of the Merchant and the Demon," "The First Old Man's Tale" deals with the step-mother who transforms her step-son into a calf and his mother into a heifer. The step-mother herself is transformed into a gazelle. "The Second Old Man's Tale" deals with the transformation of two brothers into dogs. In the last tale in "The Story of the Fisherman and the Demon," the enchanted King and his entire subjects are turned into fish. The transformation of humans into animals is

---

[124] Heckard 213
[125] Mottahedeh 31

impossible in the world of reality which draws the reader's attention to the fictionality of the stories in the text.

Character type coincidence forces the reader to question the reality of the world of the text and accept its fictionality. The presence of these extraordinary characters in *The Night* provides a means for the human imagination to soar, through language, beyond limits. At the same time, the coincidence brings a form of uncertainty of the truth of the text. These two conflicting attitudes create a unique form of relation in responding to *The Nights* very similar to relations created by highly metafictional and experimental texts of the 1960s and 70s. Reader-Response Theory of roughly the same period was a product of such metafictional representation.

The expansion of the imagination in *The Nights* is due to the absence of one definite author as it is a sort of compilation of hundreds of stories, tales, myths etc. from different periods and cultures. It is also due to its roots as a construct that carries bits and pieces in the form of tales within tales from numerous civilizations. This has given *The Nights* a sense of unbeatable appealing universality that is hard to exhaust. All readers, in some form or another, recognize some form of 'truth' of their inner hidden selves, their culture, and/or experiences in *The Nights*. With time, *The Nights* has become, as A. S. Byatt puts it, a symbol of infinity of the image of container and contained where "a character in a story invokes a character who tells a story about a character who has a story to tell... Everything proliferates."[126] Narrative proliferation in this timeless work is less modern and more postmodern and metafictional.

The Nights, with its wealth of imaginative stories, has become a universal source of inspiration for many literary figures especially during the postmodern era of the 1960s and 70s when writers and critics such as Jorge Luis Borges, John Barth, Donald Barthleme, and Thomas Pynchon felt that the possibilities of innovation in conventional narrative methods have been exhausted. During the rise of the popularity of metafictional techniques, the popularity of *The Nights* as a source of literary and imaginative inspiration has increased. The world of *The Nights* as a whole, of the device of stories within stories, and of Shahrazad the character in particular have appeared and reappeared in numerous works of fiction for centuries creating metafictional texts that are reflexive of each other and of the original text.

To further reveal the affinities of *The Nights* with metafiction, it is interesting to note that there are highly variable collections of stories in this great work. Some of *The Nights'* stories are of kings, warriors, princes, and princesses from old times reflecting high life and prestigious living such as the overall frame stories of King Shahrayar, his brother, the wazir, and Shahrazad; or the story of "The Young Woman and her Five Lovers"; or the tale of Khalifa Haroun Al Rasheed in the story of "The Porter and the Three Ladies of Baghdad"; or the tale of King Yunan in the story "The Fisherman and the Jinnee." Other stories in *The Nights* reflect the lives of the poor and their quest for living such as "The

---

[126] Byatt "Narrate or Die" xiii–xiv

Fable of the Donkey, the Ox, and the Farmer" inside *The Nights'* main frame story[127], or the story of "The Dream."[128] There are also stories which contain high and low living such as "The Sinbad Stories," "Ali Baba and the Forty Thieves," "The Tale of the Hunchback," "The Fisherman and the Jinnee," and the story "The Porter and the Three Ladies of Baghdad." This mixture between high and low is probably one of the characteristics that have kept the attractiveness of *The Nights* going on in the East and the West for centuries: "Written in a simple, almost colloquial style, and depicting a unique world of all-powerful sorcerers and ubiquitous jinn, of fabulous wealth and candid bawdry…the *Nights* is today the best known and most widely read book of authorship."[129] This simple style of writing and the high and low depiction of life (be it human, animal, or Jinn) in *The Nights* are characteristic of metafictional writing that attracted writers of metafiction such as Jorge Luis Borges and John Barth to go back to *The Nights* for inspiration. Literature during the postmodern era no longer depicts grand narratives and envisions high life and living, but it seeks to be reflective of all aspects of life and living.

In addition, high magic and superstition such as in "The Story of the Merchant and the Demon," or "The Sinbad Cycle of Stories," etc., occupy a marked space in *The Nights*. At the same time, pure humor or sheer sadness is the apparent reason for a tale or a segment in a tale such as in "The Tailor's Tale: The Young Man from Baghdad and the Barber," or "The Tale of the Second Brother Baqbaqa the Paraplegic," or "The Tale of the Third Brother, Faqfaq the Blind" which are embedded within "The Story of the Hunchback." These variations in intentional purposes behind stories and tales in *The Nights* are characteristics of metafiction that writers during the 1960s and 70s have found effective to represent the absurdity of contemporary life after the two World Wars and the threat of another that could wipe man out from Earth. A. S. Byatt stresses this point as she quotes Sir Richard Burton, one of the translators of *The Nights*, saying about this cross-cultural work:

"Every man at some term or turn of his life has longed for the supernatural powers and a glimpse of Wonderland. Here he is in the midst of it. Here he sees mighty spirits summoned to work the human mite's will, however whimsical, who can transport him in an eye-twinkling withersoever he wishes; who can ruin cities and build palaces of gold and silver, gems and jacinth…"[130]

This is one of the reasons the versatility of *The Nights* has continued to be a source of inspiration as well as source of pleasure until today.

This timeless pleasure is derived, to a large extent, from character depiction in *The Nights*. The most important characters are Shahrayar and Shahrazad. Shahrayar the character, oddly enough, is not described in *The Nights* in a realistic manner; there is no mention of his physical appearance, age, personality, or wit. His character is given depth and color by echoes and repetition of images

---

127 Dawood 20
128 Dawood 325
129 Dawood 7
130 Byatt "Narrate or Die" xiv

and events experienced by him. "He is cumulatively constructed rather than described."[131] The first frame story of *The Nights*, which "can be seen as an exploration of ideas on a theme of infidelity and betrayal, its effects and a final resolution,"[132] is important for character formation as it presents three examples of the experience of infidelity: The first is the infidelity of the queen of Shahzaman (who is presented only to illuminate the similar experience of his brother Shahryar); the character of Shahrayar becomes filled with hate when he hears of the betrayal of his brother's queen as he says: "Brother, you were fortunate in killing your wife and her lover, who gave you good reason to feel troubled, careworn, and ill… By God, had I been in your place, I would have killed at least a hundred or even a thousand women."[133] The second is the infidelity of the queen of Shahrayar which is a repetition of Shahzaman's experience of marital infidelity. When he and Shahzaman witnessed this infidelity, Shahrayar as a character is more filled with hate as he says, "No one is safe in this world. Such doing is going on in my Kingdom, and in my very palace. Perish the world and perish life."[134] To further develop the character of Shahrayar, this experience is repeated a third time in the story in the first frame narrative of *The Nights* when the two king brothers are forced to perform sex with the beautiful bride who is able to deceive the demon who stole her on her wedding night and kept her in a locked glass box in the deep ocean. With this repeated experience the character of Shahrayar develops as he says, "Brother, let us go back to our Kingdoms and our cities, never to marry a woman again. As for myself, I shall show you what I will do."[135] The repeated construction of the character Shahryar through experiences takes the method of character formation from the modern ordinary formation to the postmodern and metafictional realms.

The character of Shahrazad is similarly constructed in *The Nights* as there is no careful and detailed depiction of her appearance or her physical beauty. Again, "complexity of character is achieved through repetition, shadows, duplication, collage and indirect referral."[136] Shahrazad attracts King Shahrayar as a powerful woman capable, through the repetition of narrations, of redeeming not only herself and young women in her kingdom, but also King Shahrayar himself as she is able to free him from his culminating hate. Character construction in *The Nights* is unique and far from ordinary as it takes this classic to the meta-level of narrative where the lines between reality and fiction are so close or tightly connected. Shahrayar and Shahrazad, the two main characters, "inhabit a realm between reader and text. They are both actor and listener, teller and heroine, mirrored or figured in the tales in myriad ways, evoked in our minds by insistent reminders."[137] The relation between reader and text is intensified by

---

[131] Sallis 89
[132] Haddawy 88
[133] Haddawy 9
[134] Haddawy 11
[135] Haddawy 13
[136] Sallis 96
[137] Sallis 96

character portrayal that is more representative of metafictional portrayal of character.

Moreover, the depiction of the character Shahrazad adds to the metafictionality of this classic. *The Nights* "appears to be a story against women, but leads to the appearance of one of the strongest and cleverest heroines in world literature, who triumphs because she is endlessly inventive and keeps her head."[138] The depiction of the character Shahrazad as a wise, educated, and strong female who is able not only to redeem herself and womankind from the violence of the strong male, Shahrayar, through story-telling but also to heal Shahrayar from his hatred. This feminist stand fit for the postmodern era when minorities, women among them, fought for recognition and rights, is a very clear stand in *The Nights* of the middle ages. In this work, there is interaction between male and female, between Shahrazad and Shahrayar, based on the fact that Shahrazad is no longer a victim but a powerful female who is valuable because of her brain and not her body. Fedwa Malti-Douglas in her article, "Shahrazad Feminist," discusses the idea that Shahrazad of the Middle Ages has been transformed to represent contemporary liberated women in two examples of fiction where women are strong and capable of taking care of themselves in spite of unfavorable circumstances. The three ladies in "The Story of the Porter and the Three Ladies," or Shams al-Nahar in "The Story of Nur al-Din Ali ibn-Bakkar and the Slave-Girl Shams al-Nahar" are examples of strong capable women. Even though Shahrazad is trapped in near-death situations, she is able to narrate of willful women who take control of their lives. This demonstrates that "a tale of a powerful woman has a very different meaning when told by a trapped woman, than when it is told by a powerful woman."[139] Shahrazad of *The Nights* is so powerful a feminist that she can convince her own father, the grand wazir, of sacrificing herself to be the next bride. Also, Shahrazad "teaches by stories, and what she teaches above all justifies and exalts women and their virtues. She initiates Shahriyar into love and civilizes him."[140] She is also a feminist in her choice of not her father or another male but her sister Dunyazad, another female, to help her with her narration. Shahrazad, then, is a perfect representative of the postmodern woman/character fit for metafiction.

The popularity of *The Nights*, which started to appear in documents from the eighth century A. D. in its original language, Arabic, then in European languages after its translation beginning from the early eighteenth century, has been a factor that has displayed a tremendous implicit impact on the development of literature, then the development of literary theory in the West.[141] "The great novels of Western culture, from *Don Quixote* to *War and Peace*, from *Moby-Dick* to *Dr.*

---

[138] Byatt "The Greatest Story" 166

[139] Sallis 103

[140] Irwin *Companion* 160

[141] The translation of *The Nights* into French and English was seen "as a major literary event that transformed literary and critical norms" (Ghazoul Nocturnal Poetics 122).

Faustus, were constructed in the shadow of the one Book [*The Nights*] and its story."[142]

However, the numerous translations of *The Nights* have created not one text but several texts colored by the intentions, expertise, and angles of vision of their translators. Each of these texts provides an image of the Orient different from that in the others. Luis Parreiras-Horta in his dissertation, *Mirrors of Ink and Wonderful Lamps: The Arabian Nights in Victorian and Postmodern Literature*, discusses the effects of the different translations of *The Nights* on pre-modern and postmodern literature in the West. Parreiras-Horta gets from Edward Said's *Orientalism* that there is not "a monolithic modern discourse of the Orient in European letters that encompasses them all."[143] This is important to the metafictional debate as the adaptations of metafictional characteristics, which first appeared in *The Nights*, by Western writers differ in accordance with the angle of translation of *The Nights* an author is viewing or favoring.

Jean Antoine Galland was the first to present *The Arabian Nights*, as it has also become known, to the West from 1704 to 1717. "Galland deleted, added, and altered drastically to produce not a translation, but a French adaptation, or rather a work of his creation."[144] Richard Burton, himself a translator of *The Nights*, calls Galland's translation a "delightful abbreviation and adaptation."[145] In spite of that, Galland's translation has played a big and effective role in the development of literature. The notable metafictionist, Jorge Luis Borges says, "Galland establishes the canon." Borges adds that the happiest and most felicitous praise of *The 1001 nights*—from Coleridge, De Quincey, Standhal, Tennyson, Edgar Allan Poe, Newman—comes from readers of Galland's translation. Two hundred years and ten better translations have come and gone, but that man of Europe or the Americas who thinks of *The 1001 Nights* thinks invariably of that first translation.[146]

The translation of Galland has not only affected individual authors but it has also affected the whole movement of literature. Borges says:

"Galland publishes his first volume in 1704. It produces a sort of scandal, but at the same time it enchants the rational France of Louis XIV. When we think of the Romantic Movement, we usually think of dates that are much later. But it might be said that the Romantic Movement begins at the moment when someone, in Normandy or in Paris, reads *The Thousand and One Nights*. He leaves the world legislated by Boileau and enters the world of Romantic freedom."[147]

The translation of *The Nights* by Edward William Lane in 1839 is also heavily edited and loaded with notes. Borges calls Lane a 'virtuoso of subterfuge' as Lane in his translation "justifies his interpretation of every

---

[142] Byatt "Narrate or Die" xx

[143] Parreiras-Horta 7

[144] Haddawy xix–xx

[145] Burton xxviii

[146] Borges "The Translators of the 1001 Nights" 74

[147] Borges *Seven Nights* 54

doubtful word."[148] Lane's translation is faithful in showing the exact nature of the Islamic culture, and those authors affected by his translation did not empty *The Nights* of its association with the Islamic culture of reality. In spite of that, Borges says, "It is very well known that they [Galland and Lane] disinfected the *Nights*,"[149] hinting that Burton's translation is the one which infected this great classic.

Richard Burton's translation of *The Nights* is contaminated with him. Burton, the prolific writer, "was a man who had much to say, and seventy-two volumes of his work go on saying it."[150] In his translation of *The Nights*, "Burton is interested in the exotic, the quaint, and the colorful,"[151] and this interest has continued to influence readers of this classic until recently. Although Burton's translation and other translations of *The Nights* were quite popular, the need for fresh translations never ceased, which is a sign of the durability and flexibility of this masterpiece. "It seems that it was constructed in such a way as to allow and even invite radical changes in its content, yet at the same time preserve its own internal logic."[152] The translations of *The Nights*, therefore, created different texts than the original, which have been playing significant roles in the shaping of the literary consciousness in the West. Ferial Ghazoul says:

"It is important to understand that the variation in texts is not an accident due to inadequate transmission, but is rather a fundamental aspect of the narrative performance of *The Arabian Nights* and an intimate characteristic of the received texts."[153]

This characteristic of the received text of Burton, in particular, has affected the Movement of the Decadents who celebrated the notion of "Art for Art's sake." The movement of the Decadents came after the Romantic Movement and before the Modernist Movement, and consequently, "The Modernists inherited from the Decadents an *Arabian Nights* emptied of any intended correspondence with reality."[154] In general, in the English translations of *The Nights* performed during the nineteenth-century there is, according to Parreiras-Horta, "a broad trend away from the Enlightenment reconciliation of reason and magic…to the conscious disengagement with truth claims and embrace of artifice."[155] The nineteenth-century translations of *The Nights*, Burton's translation in particular, and the Decadents' view of aesthetic are primarily what color the metafiction of John Barth.

In its own birth place, *The Nights* has been neglected and pushed to a shadow for centuries. It looked, especially during the modernist period, like a haphazard collection of short tales. However, the marvelous structure of this timeless work

---

[148] Borges "The Translators of the 1001 Nights" 75-76
[149] Borges "The Translators of the 1001 Nights" 76
[150] Borges "The Translators of the 1001 Nights" 77
[151] Haddawy xxvii
[152] Ghazoul *Nocturnal Poetics* 4
[153] Ghazoul *Nocturnal Poetics* 4
[154] Parreiras-Horta 8
[155] Parreiras-Horta, 8

has been drawing more attention in the West first and then in the East with the abandonment of modernist narrative techniques and the adaptation of postmodernist styles of writing fiction. Due to this change of views concerning narrative presentation, the popularity of *The Nights* as a fine and timeless work of narrative art has increased tremendously since the middle of the twentieth century. The narrative art in *The Nights* has been a source of inspiration for major writers of metafiction such as Borges, Barth, Rushdie, Byatt, and others. Also, there is in the West and in the East a growing number of academic studies that discuss novel narrative techniques. These studies usually take innovation in fiction back to dates much earlier than what has generally been proposed.[156]

Also, there are other factors that have helped in reviving contemporary interest in *The Nights*. Globalization, which erased major spatial and temporal differences, have helped in renewing interest in *The Nights* as the growing number of creative and academic works associated with *The Nights* take no time to reach readers across the globe. The emergence of new trends in literary studies such as metafiction, poststructuralism, cultural criticism, and cultural studies (Edward Said's *Orientalism* in particular) have been directing attention to *The Nights* with its intricate and complex structure fit for the contemporary style of narration. Developments in science, namely chaos theory, with their fairly recent recognition of the importance of human action as part of a dynamic system in changing one's path in life; of the importance of initial conditions as directing forces of action; and of celebrating complexity have brought *The Nights*, which has all these characteristics, into contemporary interest.

I hope that after the previous discussions, it becomes apparent that in *The Nights* there is a practice of a highly sophisticated form of narrative art long before this kind of the so-called postmodernist writing was identified as metafiction. There is, in this classic, a clear awareness of readers (or listeners) and their possible response to fiction long before reader response theory became a prominent influence in literary studies. The fiction of *The Nights*, then, undoubtedly, is a precursor to postmodern fiction writing.

To conclude this chapter, it is appropriate to say that the rise and frequent use of the techniques of metafiction in contemporary literature coincide to a large degree with the growing presence of references to *The Nights* in numerous important contemporary literary works in the West. This coincidence points to the possible relationship between the two, *The Nights* and metafiction. It is a relationship that has not been fully acknowledged by literary theorists and critics. Most theorists and critics did not yet consider *The Nights* a vital component that constitutes a corner stone of the origin of metafiction in literature.

---

[156] For example, Parreiras-Hort's dissertation, *Mirrors of Ink and Wonderful Lamps: The Arabian Nights in Victorian and Postmodern Literature*, Kobler's dissertation, "Postmodern Narrative Techniques in the Work of Nathaniel Hawthorne: Metafiction, Fabulation, and Hermenutical Semiosis", and Ghazoul's books, *The Arabian Nights: A Structural Analysis* and *Nocturnal Poetics: The Arabian Nights in Contemporary Context* take the start of innovation in fiction much earlier than the 1960s and 1970s.

Chapter II
Development and Theorization of Metafiction

This chapter deals with the development, theorization, and characteristics of experimentation in literature that came to be termed as metafiction. In order to have a complete view of metafiction, this chapter has a chronological presentation of several fictional and nonfictional works by pioneering writers whose texts show either development or applications of metafictional techniques. Along with that, this chapter includes the discussion of several critical works that helped in the theorization of metafiction. The characteristics of metafiction will be dealt with through the discussion of these fictional and critical works. This chapter concludes with raising the issue of the possibility of including *The Nights* as one of the earliest examples that show obvious characteristics of metafiction.

The 1960s witnessed a sharp increased interest in abandoning the traditional writing techniques that prevailed during the realist and modernist periods and adopting new techniques that were unusual in the West. In an attempt to reflect the uncertain realties of the world and acquire a personal and collective meaning of existence, writers have steadily become interested in self-conscious expression by using unconventional and experimental techniques that operate on two levels: the level of text and the level of the reader.

On the level of text, plots no longer mattered for writers, and they concentrated instead on producing texts that were open-ended with possibilities of infinite numbers of interpretations. Writers found a way to enrich their works through opening new channels within their fiction. They felt the need to display reflexivity; of relying on myths, folklore, works of fiction, characters, or even writing methods to help them reflect the world or read it as text. Writers forced implicit or explicit aspects of literary theory and criticism into their texts as signs of novelty, creativity, and rejection of formal representation. The West after World War II and through the Cold War years was transformed into a different kind of reality that shook its stability, and conventional writing methods were no longer applicable and appropriate to represent that instability. Writers moved their techniques from concentrating mainly on the text to also concentrating on the reader as an important element for the interpretation of the text and the construction of reality.

Writers sought to challenge modern modes of writing narratives by intruding to converse with characters or explain a situation. They even address the reader directly in an attempt to engage the reader with the text. Language in the hands of writers became a playing instrument to show simplicity or even naivety in order to force the reader to rethink of other levels of interpretation. This type of parody reflects authors' attempts to reveal the absurdity of the world after two world wars and a threat of another major world war that could drive man to extinction.

All these deviations from the accepted norms of writing fiction that prevailed during the realist and modern periods had to have roots that might not be quite apparent during these times of change. However, the following few decades of experimentation, more studies have been dating the start of experimentation in literature in general to earlier than what has been commonly viewed. A review of some of the studies available in the West concerning the development, theorization, and nature of metafiction or experimentation shows that there are yet other possibilities of recognizing more works that contain elements of metafiction.

The PhD dissertation of Rachel Roth Chiguluri, *The Burden of History in the Contemporary Novel: National Pain and Narrative Techniques*,[157] is a study that takes the roots of the change of perception of things that led to metafiction back to the Age of Enlightenment. Chiguluri takes the subject of the study of history as her entry into writing in general. She says "The writing of history served as a means of inquiring into the nature of man and man's place in the universe."[158] Chiguluri adds:

"The writing of history did indeed undergo important transformations during this time, beginning with a rejection of the annalistic and chronological methods practiced during the previous century. With the theories developed by John Locke about the human mind and cognition, and with the impact of the scientific revolution in general, this is the time when the study of man was made into a science."[159]

Chiguluri extends the effect of the Enlightenment with her emphasis on eighteenth century thought with the philosophy of Immanuel Kant in his work *Kritik* when she explains what he meant by human experience. "An essential aspect of Kant's theory is the distinction he makes between 'things as they appear to be' and 'things in themselves.'"[160] Chiguluri thinks that *Kritik* provides a new perspective for understanding "human nature, specifically man's capacity for knowledge, action, and aesthetic judgment."[161] Although *Kritik* is pure philosophy, it has ideas that may have provided the spark that led writers of fiction to stress on the fictionality of their texts. Michael Davidson in his review of Larry McCaffery's book, *The Metafictional Muse*, supports Chiguluri's reference of the start of metafiction to Kant's philosophy. Davidson says,

---

[157] Rachel Roth Chiguluri's study, done in 2001, is one of a growing number of studies which participate in viewing reality through a look at history and how it is depicted in fiction

[158] Chiguluri 8

[159] Chiguluri 7

[160] Chiguluri 12

[161] 12

"McCaffrey sees the metafictional impulse as originating in the Kantian philosophical revolution with its belief in the creative imagination and its emphasis on the mediating function of subjectivity."[162] The Enlightenment expressed through Kant's view of human experience could be the base, according to Western views, of what later became one of the most important characteristics in the construction of contemporary fiction: There is no fixed meaning; all meaning is subject to individual perception. Meaning is multiple and contextual. In other words, there are no stable realities since experiences of an individual define the way s/he perceives the world. However, Chiguluri did not acknowledge that *The Nights*, which this book proposes has definite metafictional characteristics, has any effect on the development of fiction even though it reached the West, through translation, in 1704. It appears though that it is not only the Enlightenment and philosophies produced during that period that has made a difference. The Western readers' reception of Eastern texts has contributed in changing Western thought.

Sheila Frazier Kobler's dissertation, *Postmodern Narrative Techniques in the Work of Nathaniel Hawthorne: Metafiction, Fabulation, and Hermeneutical Semiosis* (1993), is important to this study as it locates early metafictional techniques in fiction in Hawthorne's works of the nineteenth century in particular.[163] Kobler presents a thorough study of Hawthorne's connection to metafiction. Critics, Kobler says, think that "Hawthorne's art falls off after his nearly perfect work, *The Scarlet Letter.*"[164] Kobler explains that critics have seen *The House of the Seven Gables, The Blithedale Romance*, and *The Marble Faun* as "structurally flawed or deficient."[165] Critics misunderstood Hawthorne's strangely structured works, Kobler argues, because

"Hawthorne's fiction is a fiction that is in itself an act of deconstructing the text of the universe. Readers observe him in the act of reading/writing his story and are thereby instructed how to approach his re-created puzzle or riddle of the universe by becoming readers/writers along with him."[166]

Hawthorne's works, according to Kobler, show the metafictional characteristics of self-reflexivity where the author is aware of the act of writing as he stresses on the fictionality of his work, as well as being aware of his reader's participation in the creation of meaning. Hawthorne's works, says Kobler,

"reveal a close affinity to writers of the Nouveau roman such as Jean-Paul Sartre, Michel Butor, Andre Gide, and Alain Robbe-Grillet, who assert the

---

[162] Michael Davidson 484

[163] Sheila Frazier Kobler, in the introduction to her dissertation, acknowledges that G. R. Thomson's *The Art of Authorial Presence: Hawthorne's Provincial Tales* (1993) is the first work that links Hawthorne's work to postmodernity

[164] Kobler, 8

[165] Kobler, 8

[166] Kobler 13

importance of the reader's role in the creation of the novel. Sartre claims, 'there is art only for and through another.'"[167]

Hawthorne's works reveal yet another metafictional characteristic of playfulness. "It requires an energetic, imaginative reader willing to enter into the artistic game of the fabulator, not depending on highly developed characters or intricate plots to provide pleasure."[168] Also, Hawthorne's works, as Kobler explains, celebrate subjectivity, human experience, and creativity which are characteristics of metafiction. Kobler says:

"Possibly most of Hawthorne's art can be understood as one large metaphor of his experience of life, as he constantly interpreted the meaning of his art in relationship to life, which explains the many artists, art forms, and art objects we find in his short tales and his romances."[169]

By including real artists, art forms, and art objects into his fictional realms, Hawthorne in the nineteenth century was blurring the boundaries of fact and fiction, which is certainly another characteristic of metafiction. In addition, Kobler has found in Hawthorne's fiction an affinity with the Eastern narrative style, but says that most critics "have shown no interest in Eastern influence on Hawthorne belittling the importance, formal or thematic, of the story cycles and apologues of the East..."[170] In spite of Kobler's recognition of the Eastern story cycle on Hawthorne whose work shows metafictional tendencies according to her, she does not refer to *The Nights*, one of the leading works with the story cycle, as metafictional.

Edgar Allan Poe's "The Thousand-and-Second Tale of Scheherazade" is also a nineteenth century short story that shows Western admiration of an Eastern story cycle; Poe's story is self-reflexive of *The Nights* as it is a story about the fate of Shahrazad the story-teller. Poe's other work, *Tales of the Grotesque and Arabesque* (1840), is a totally Western framed-tale collection of tales which mixes between themes of mystery, comedy, and terror. It is a collection that celebrates the arabesque, which in turn is acknowledged by John Barth who made the connection between metafiction and the arabesque in 1991.[171]

In the twentieth century, literary figures have been moved by philosophical thoughts. For example, the French Michel Foucault and Jacques Derrida, the Russian Mikhail Bakhtin, and the American Hayden White all prominently offer new methodologies for pursuing knowledge and ascertaining truth. Each of these critics, in his own way, subverts the dominant—in other words, Western— discourses that had stood as foundational pillars of a set of knowledge and, by so doing, each postulates new theories and proposes alternative methods of arriving at truth or defining reason.[172]

---

[167] Kobler 14

[168] Kobler 14

[169] Kobler 15

[170] Kobler 270–271

[171] John Barth *Further Fridays* 321

[172] Chiguluri 38

This is probably why Eastern fictions have not been acknowledged as sources of innovation as they are not parts of the Western literary canon.

The experimentalists whose styles were later theorized as metafiction, have, therefore been influenced by Kant, Foucault, Derrida, Bakhtin and White.[173] The metafictionists are convinced that there is no set truth in history; there are personal and local truths reported or written in accordance with cultural pressures. Language is a verbal construct that carries the personal experience and observations of its writer. The reader forms meaning in accordance with his own beliefs, psychological state of mind, and cultural settings.

As a reaction to such philosophies and structural innovations, experimentation in literature started after World War II as a trend in the construction of fiction. In France, French structuralists have come up, in the 1950s, with the nouveau roman, or the French new novel which was a divergence from the modern classical style of writing novels. Nouveau roman showed interest in individuality of vision rather than stressing on character and plot. Works of writers such as Alain Robbe-Grillet, Claude Simon, Michel Buter, and Marguerite Duras show novel narrative techniques that no longer rely on omniscient narrators or pay much attention to time and space. Language itself became an essential element in the creation of meaning and representation of culture; free play of language took texts away from reality and into irreality. These works also show the writers' occupations with the reader as the sole interpreter of a text. Fictions with metafictional techniques influenced by such thought dominated during the 1960s and 1970s. However, such philosophical influences did not continue to direct the metafictional flow, a point that will be discussed later.

During the 1950s, the fiction of the Argentinean Jorge Luis Borges[174] reveals signs of experimentation that John Barth refers to as "the metaphysical disturbances of Borges' fiction."[175] Borges' fiction and non-fiction show new philosophical as well as structural literary applications. Borges' contemporary engagement with the philosophical and ontological elements in his reading of the 602nd night of *The Nights* has paved the way in the West for the renewed interest of not only philosophy in *The Nights* but also of its structure as suitable devices in the construction of contemporary narratives. Evelyn Fishburn says about Borges' engagement with *The Nights*, "Borges has declared the *Arabian Nights* not an exotic other but a constitutive component of our culture, part of our

---

[173] The ideas of those philosophers have also helped in the emergence of post-structuralism, which also rejects absolute truth, and rejects the author as a central figure in the formation of meaning. Post-structuralism also calls for meta language where language is used extraordinarily for referential purposes. Through these three areas, post-structuralism and metafiction meet

[174] "Perhaps the most striking characteristic of his [Borges] writings is their extreme intellectual reaction against all the disorder and contingency of immediate reality, their radical insistence on breaking with the given world and postulating another" (*Introduction to Labyrinths: Selected Stories & Other Writings* xiii).

[175] Barth, *Friday Book* 69

memory."[176] Several of Borges' stories contain references to *The Nights*: 'Tlon, Uqbar, Orbis Tertius,' 'The Zahir,' 'The Garden of Forking Paths,' 'Brodie's Report,' 'The Book of Sands,' and 'The Man on the Threshold.' Partially because of Borges, *The Nights* was reintroduced to the West not as an Eastern but a Western text, which further denies *The Nights* its Eastern origin.

During the 1950s, Borges' fiction shows what was later considered characteristics of metafiction. He challenges the reader's sense of reality by introducing elements of magic and myth, and self-consciously questions the role of the narrative within the terms of its constructability. "In his fiction, Borges often blurs the lines between history and fiction, privileging language as a product of the imagination over a so-called empirical reality."[177] Borges' short story "Averroes' Search" introduces the reader to the narrator's realities of a well-known Muslim scholar, Ibn Rushd, and to Islamic culture through fiction.

Borges is also a pioneer in the method of self-reflexivity where a writer subverts an existing work of fiction in accordance with his own understanding of it. Borges practiced what later was known as an important characteristic of metafiction by rewriting already existing works of fiction by well-known authors in Europe and the United States, such as Virginia Woolf, Rudyard Kipling, Walt Whitman, Herman Melville, William Faulkner, and Jack London, among others. "Borges' recreations of these authors' works foreground one of the main ideas explored in his fiction, that new readings of texts evolve with a changing reality."[178]

During the early 1950s in North America, the young John Barth who worked at the time in the Classics Library at Johns Hopkins, filing books, became absorbed in reading literature. He became enchanted not mostly with Western fiction but with the ancient Eastern story cycle. *The Nights* and the arabesque became important components of his fiction. In 1990, Barth says the arabesque is "centered on the playful treatment of artistic form."[179] In his article, "4 1/2 Lectures: The Arabesque," Barth discusses Friedrich von Schlegel's notion of arabesque by saying:

"The arabesque...characteristically involves the rupture of illusion by references in the text to its author, to the process of writing, and so forth; the transgression of the boundary between the reality of reader and author and the reality of the characters and world of the text; privileging of the 'interplay between and among norms, forms, voices, themes, and languages...' Authorial self-reference in the Schlegelian arabesque is particularly problematical because the author behind the text also *is* the text."[180]

Barth's preoccupation with *The Nights* and what he termed 'the genre of arabesque' represented for him in the 1960s and 70s "an oasis from the narratives of political disenchantment in contemporary American fiction...the *Nights*

---

[176] Evelyn Fishburn, 213
[177] Chiguluri 50
[178] Chiguluri 50
[179] Barth *Further Fridays* 321
[180] Barth *Further Fridays* 321

formed the principal point of reference for Barth as he argued for a form of literature that emphasized formal experimentation rather than concerns about novelty of content."[181] Barth was also occupied with the narrative style of Borges who in turn was enchanted by *The Nights* and its narrative style.

While Barth was partially occupied with the narrative construction of *The Nights*, literary experimentations in France and Argentina most likely influenced the development of metafiction elsewhere as in 1962 Vladimir Nabokov published his novel *Pale Fire*. This work contains some of the most important metafictional characteristics that differ from those found in other works of the period. *Pale Fire* has an untraditional structure: the lines between literary genres (between narrative, poetry, and autobiography) are not defined, its author deliberately draws attention to the fictional nature of the work, and the two fictional authors of the novel are central characters in the novel. *Pale Fire*, therefore, has a unique structure in that it is written as a 999-line poem in four cantos. The title of the novel is self-reflexive in that it is taken from Shakespeare's *Timon of Athens*: "The moon's an errant thief, / And her pale fire she snatches from the sun" (Act IV, scene 3). This line is a metaphor about creativity and inspiration. *Pale Fire* looks like a long autobiography of the fictional author and it contains an introduction and commentary by a fictional editor. These metafictional characteristics were, at the time, totally unusual and innovative.

After *Pale Fire* and in 1963 came another metafictional novel, Thomas Pynchon's *V.*, that contains several characteristics of metafiction that resemble those in *Pale Fire*: a speculative title, an unusual structure, and a blurring line between the genres of novel and short story. Pynchon's title, *V.* is a mysterious entity and a character that another central character searches for. V. remains unidentified until the end of the novel. The mysteriousness of V. represents a dilemma and Pynchon invites his reader to participate in the deciphering and identification of his central character. Also, the structure of Pynchon's novel is unusual with two storylines that increasingly converge to form a V-shape. Moreover, the almost 500 pages of *V.* contain other typographical devices such as different size scripts and asterisks etc. *V.* is a novel that seems like a short-story collection because of the several independent narratives that constitute it.

In spite of these obvious metafictional characteristics, Nabokov's novel and Pynchon's novel were not taken to be metafictional novels simply because metafiction had not yet been theorized as such. An interesting early review of *V.* written in the *New York Times* in 1963 shows how the literary milieu received *V.*:

Such novels are invariably lengthy, heavily populated with eccentrics, deviates, grotesques with funny names (so they can be remembered), and are usually composed of a series of bizarre adventures or episodes in which the central character is involved, then removed and flung abruptly into another. Very often a Quest is incorporated, which keeps the central character on the move.[182]

---

[181] Luis Paulo Parreiras-Horta 139
[182] George Plimpton nil

Plimpton calls Pynchon's style of writing in *V.* picaresque, where the author "can string together the short stories he has at hand." Moreover, the author "can afford to take chances, to be excessive, even prolix, knowing that in a work of great length stretches of doubtful value can be excused."[183] These early views of the experimental metafiction of the 1960s foresaw the death of such radical experimentations as authors of fiction turned away to a more structured experimentation, later theorized as metafiction, similar to that in *The Nights*.

Experimentation in literature was the subject of a critical book published in 1963. Mia I. Gerhardt's book, *The Art of Story-Telling: a Literary Study of the Thousand and One Nights*, is probably the first critical work that takes innovation in literature right back to *The Nights*. Gerhardt proposes to study the art of story-telling in *The Nights* from the view point of the literary criticism of the 1960s. She hopes the results of her study "could contribute something to solving the secrets of the deceptively simple art of story-telling."[184] The author, therefore, acknowledges the deceptive simplicity of the art of story-telling in *The Nights*. Years later, this deceptive simplicity won the scene of creative writing style over the highly experimental style of writing in for example *Pale Fire* and *V.*

In 1965, John Barth, who became a professor of creative writing and a well-known author, published his essay "Muse, Spare Me," and then in 1967 and 1980 he published his other two influential essays "The Literature of Exhaustion" and "The Literature of Replenishment." Overall, these three essays show some aspects of the development of metafiction in the USA. In "Muse, Spare Me," Barth expresses his devotion to Shahrazad and *The Nights*:

"When I think of my condition and my hope, musewise, in the time between now and when I shall run out of ink or otherwise expire, it is Scheherazade who comes to mind, for many reasons—not least of which is a technical interest in the ancient device of the framing-story, used more beautifully in the *Nights* than anywhere else I know."[185]

In "Muse, Spare Me," Barth approaches his muse in order to take the processes of constructing narratives from the realities and fears of the 1960s into the fictious world of the muse. "I say, Muse, spare me…from social-historical responsibility, and in the last analysis from every other kind as well, except artistic."[186] Authors of fiction, Barth thinks, should take the example Shahrazad of *The Nights* who deals with her realities and fears through story-telling.

Since the 1960s, Barth has been going back to the past and using *The Nights* more often than any other work in search of models from the past to present the postmodern metafiction of the present; Shahrazad, the character, appears in Barth's fiction more often than any other character in his entire fiction. In spite of the heavy presence of Shahrazad in his fiction, Barth says in his article, "Tales Within Tales Within Tales," that "it was never Scheherazade's stories that

---

[183] Plimpton nil

[184] Mia Gerhardt 6. Gerhardt's book has no mention of metafiction simply because metafiction in the early 1960s had not been theorized as such

[185] Barth *Friday Book* 57

[186] Barth *Friday Book* 55

seduced and beguiled me, but their teller and the extraordinary circumstances of their telling: in other words, the character and situation of Scheherazade and the narrative convention of the framing story."[187] Barth, therefore, has been fascinated with the metafictional characteristics in *The Nights*. During the 1960s, *The Nights* represented for Barth an oasis from the narratives of political disenchantment in contemporary American fiction delivered by writers concerned with the Viet Nam War, political protest, desegregation, and the rise of feminism. Against this background of political and social turmoil, *The Nights* formed the principal point of reference for Barth as he argued for a form of literature that emphasized formal experimentation rather than concerns about novelty of content.[188]

Although Barth has been exploiting *The Nights* in the construction of his metafictional works for decades, almost no prominent critic or writer, other than Borges, has done the same.

In 1967, John Barth published, in *The Atlantic Monthly*, his famous essay "The Literature of Exhaustion" which is "emblematic of the new trends in American fiction in the late sixties."[189] Barth's essay has been, since its publication, very influential in the debate of metafiction or experimentation in literature. In it, Barth openly discusses the intricate narrative style of *The Nights* through his recognition of Borges' use of night 602, which is supposedly a story from *The Nights*, the inexhaustible narrative. Barth discusses the as yet unclear signs of experimentation in the construction of narrative fiction and he explains what he means by exhaustion by saying: "By 'exhaustion' I don't mean anything so tired as the subject of physical, moral, or intellectual decadence, only the used-upness of certain forms or the felt exhaustion of certain possibilities—by no means necessarily a cause for despair."[190] In "The Literature of Exhaustion," Barth praises Borges' fiction as it illustrates "how an artist may paradoxically turn the felt ultimacies of our time into material and means for his work."[191] Years later, in 1993, Barth writes in his article, "Borges and I: a Mini Memoir" about "The Literature of Exhaustion," saying that the "essay (with its much misunderstood title) was my attempt to articulate, with Sr. Borges' assistance, what I saw going on round about me and felt in my aesthetic bones in the American High Sixties."[192] In this article, Barth pays tribute to Jorge Luis Borges and his ontological treatment of fiction, as Barth "approaches Borges with a distinct set of epistemological assumptions regarding the role of fiction which

---

[187] Barth *Friday Book* 220

[188] Parreiras-Horta 139. In Parreiras-Horta's study of *The Nights* done in 2004, he says, "the Nights tales are not mere accounts of miracles but rather…announcements of the miraculous advent of justice" (2). Barth, in the 1960s, might have been aware of the implications of justice in these tales

[189] Susana Isabel Araujo 108

[190] Barth *Friday Book* 64

[191] Barth *Friday Book* 71

[192] Barth *Further Fridays* 169

stress the ends of literary inquiry rather than those of philosophy."[193] Borges, according to Barth in the article *"refuses* to write an 'original' text, instead producing a meta-text, a pseudo-learned commentary on *other* texts—texts which exist, however, only in his own imagination."[194] In the "Literature of Exhaustion," Barth praises Borges' works as being excellent works of art; "they illustrate in a simple way the difference between the *fact* of aesthetic ultimacies and their artistic *use.* What it comes to is that an artist doesn't merely exemplify an ultimacy; he employs it."[195] Barth acknowledges Borges for devising a strategy for exemplifying and exploiting the concept of 'literary exhaustion'…drawing the notion that no writer can possibly add to the sum of original literature to produce remarkable and original works of fiction. Barth contrasts the 'technically up to date' writers such as Borges with the work of those artists who for better or for worse write not as if the twentieth century didn't exist, but as if the great writers of the last sixty years or so hadn't existed.[196]

Brian McHale, in his book *Constructing Postmodernism* gives his understanding of Barth's appreciation of Borges and his (Barth's) view of fiction in his famous article saying:

"Exhausted literature can be replenished by reviving the traditional ('pre-modernist,' says Barth) value of fiction. But, to be valid, such resurrection cannot be mere retrogression to the poetics of Balzac, Flaubert, Dostoevsky, Tolstoy. No more than anything else can fiction go home again; the old values must be revived in a way which takes the twentieth century into account. Postmodernist fiction must transcend the antitheses of modernist and pre-modernist writing, keeping 'one foot always in the narrative past…and one foot in, one might say, the Parisian structuralist present.'"[197]

Throughout his "Literature of Exhaustion," Barth does not refer to The Nights or to Borges' fondness of *The Nights* as possible sources of metanarrative or metafiction.

Years later, in 1980, Barth explains in his other famous essay, "The Literature of Replenishment" that in 1966/67 terms for innovation in literature were not yet established. Barth says, however,

"a number of us [writers and critics], in quite different ways and with varying combinations of intuitive response and conscious deliberation, were already well into the working out, not of the next best thing after modernism, but the best next thing: what is gropingly now called postmodernist fiction; what I hope might also be thought of one day as a literature of replenishment."[198]

"The Literature of Replenishment," puts many responsibilities on the shoulders of the author as creator of a literary work. The article celebrates the

---

[193] Parreiras-Horta 143

[194] Brian McHale 27

[195] Barth *Friday Book* 68

[196] Araujo 108

[197] McHale 27

[198] Barth *Friday Book* 206

metafictional characteristic of self-reflexivity as it idealizes the creative author as someone who makes use of the literature of the past in order to reinterpret the present. It "returns to the idea that the way forward in narrative was to go backwards in search of an 'old' form which could be rejuvenated."[199] In his dissertation, Ernst Sebastian Hierl presents the same idea as he says:

"Through his reorchestration of Greek mythology and especially of Shahrazad stories of *The Thousand and One Nights*, Barth attempts to illustrate his ideal of a postmodern literature that combines tradition and contemporary concerns, to form a literature of replenishment that appeals to both the average and the academic reader."[200]

John Barth, the writer and critic who is also one of those who revived metafiction, does not limit metafiction to a certain period of time. In an interview with Barth, he [Barth] says, "Fiction about fiction, stories about storytelling, have an ancient history."[201] What is special about Barth in the metafictional debate is that he is an academic author who holds a postgraduate degree in creative writing and spent all his life teaching at a university and pursuing an academic career. He has full knowledge of the whole literary canon from Homer to the present completed by the major critical figures from Existentialism to post-structuralism in his texts and essays. As an example of his early extensive knowledge of both theory and practice, Barth uses self-reflexivity in discussing his literary options in his story "Title" in *Lost in the Funhouse.*[202] This story represents Barth's attempt to translate his theoretic demands of his famous essay "The Literature of Exhaustion" into fiction. Barth's "Title" reveals his understanding of the state of literature, which he believes to have exhausted traditional means of representation and to have come to a dead end.

The year 1968 witnessed the publication of two important metafictional works, John Barth's *Lost in the Funhouse* and William Gass's *Willie Masters' Lonesome Wife.* Barth's work, which represents another example of self-reflexivity, of mixing theory of fiction with practice of fiction, is a collection of fourteen short stories with the title of one of them as the overall title for the whole collection. The short stories of *Lost in the Funhouse* are "studies in ontology and aesthetics which offer portraits of the artist as existentialist intellectual becoming philosophical analyst of world culture."[203] Much of *Lost in the Funhouse* "deals explicitly with fictional techniques and experiments in narration."[204] The immediate success and growing popularity of *Lost in the Funhouse* reveal popular preoccupation with a narrative technique of fiction that is about fiction; be it another fiction or the process of writing fiction as is the case in *Lost in the Funhouse.* Fiction about fiction is the most obvious characteristic of metafiction.

---

[199] Richard Bradbury 61

[200] Hierl 49

[201] William Plumley 9

[202] Barth *Lost in the Funhouse* 104

[203] Jac Tharpe

[204] Tharpe 10

William Gass's 1968 novel *Willie Masters' Lonesome Wife* was, when first published, another experimental creation that attracted readers and critics that year. Gass's novel has no clear plot, and it deals with language in general and words in particular not only in a literary sense but also in a philosophical sense. The self-conscious narrator deals more with his relationship to his fictional work than with other characters in the novel. This technique of the preoccupation with the process of writing itself, which years later was recognized as a metafictional characteristic, directs the reader's attention to the author's intended meaning behind such a technique. "Indeed, the narrator of the work—the 'Lonesome Wife' of the title—is that lady language herself."[205] *Willie Masters' Lonesome Wife*, therefore, deals with the building blocks of fiction—words and concepts—in a more direct and sophisticated fashion than most other metafictions; it is more explicitly experimental than just about any other work of fiction.[206]

The metafictional elements in *Willie Masters' Lonesome Wife* resemble those in other experimental novels like Nabokov's *Pale Fire*, Pynchon's *V.*, and Barth's *Lost in the Funhouse*. During the 1960s, narration was a favored, perhaps *the* favored, object of experimentation in literature that characterizes a large number of texts from the period.

In 1969, Robert Coover published *Pricksongs and Descants* where two short stories, "The Brother," and "J's Marriage," are especially important to the debate of metafiction, as both deal with well-known stories of religious connotations. In "The Brother," the character Noah says to his brother who is building a great ark, "It don't matter none your work."[207] This signifies that a great majority of people in the West, in the 1960s, were questioning grand religious narratives. This questioning of grand narratives is another characteristic of metafiction. Coover in "The Brother" is "interested in the suffering of the everyday people who were left behind to drown, who are given such scant mention in the scripture."[208] In "J's Marriage," Coover also looks at common religious beliefs from another perspective as he mixes the phenomenon of the birth of Christ with the feelings of the people around Mary who were not able (in the Western belief) to comprehend the miracle. "Coover's intention here is not to be sacrilegious but to cut through the muck and reveal what such a situation would mean in individual human terms."[209] The metafictional elements of dealing with grand narratives in these two stories might have influenced Salman Rushdie's *The Satanic Verses* (1988).

The prevalence of experimentation in fiction at the end of the 1960s led to the theorization of that experimentation as 'fabulation.' Robert Scholes, one of the literary critics most concerned with the techniques of experimental writing, or fabulation, says that the fabulator "is important to the extent that he can rejoice us, and his ability to produce joy and peace depends on the skill with which he

---

[205] Larry McCaffery 24
[206] McCaffery "The Art of Metafiction" 23
[207] Robert Coover *Pricksongs and Descants* 97
[208] Margaret Heckard 219
[209] Heckard 220

fabulates…of all narrative form, fabulation puts the highest premium on art and joy."[210] Scholes also thinks that the technique of structure highlights the fabulator as the highest authority in forming a work of fiction. The self-consciousness of the role of the writer in his concentration on designing a text also invites the reader to take part in the construction of meaning intended behind the text. That represented the core of experimentation in literature during the 1960s. Fabulation, which was almost the first English term that referred to experimentation in literature during the late 1960s, did not continue to be popular since it concentrated on the role of the fabulator as key element in the construction of fiction. Fabulation was replaced by Metafiction, the term that gives equal attention to writer of text, text itself, reader of text, and language as medium of expression of any text.

Fabulation was replaced by metafiction when William Gass coined the term 'metafiction' in 1970 in his article, "Philosophy and the Form of Fiction." Gass in this article is opposing critics who labeled any unusual fiction as an anti-novel, and says, "There are metatheorems in mathematics and logic, ethics has its linguistic oversoul, everywhere lingos to converse about lingos are being contrived, and the case is no different in the novel…many of the so-called anti-novels are really metafictions."[211] Gass, according to Larry McCaffery, "is making a subtle but much needed distinction between anti-novels and metafictions."[212] McCaffery explains that subtle distinction saying:

"By 1970 a certain type of work had begun to appear with insistent regularity, clearly belonging to the anti-novel tradition but maintaining a distinct unity of intention, approach, and subject matter. These works, represented by Donald Barthelme's *Snow White* (1967), John Barth's *Lost in the Funhouse* (1968), Robert Coover's *Pricksongs and Descants* (1969), and Ronald Sukenick's *Up* (1970), are all highly self-conscious works which deal directly with the inadequacies and problems of current fiction writing. Akin to Beckett's self-ruminating narratives and owing even more to the cerebral, intensely literary creations of Borges and Nabokov, these works also derived from the meta-theorems being developed in many other disciplines. Like the meta-theorist, the metafictionist had seen that only by creating a new form with its own referential language could he deal effectively with his original subject—fiction making."[213]

The term metafiction, therefore, involves the expanding, through language, of the consciousness of writers and readers in order for writers to express themselves and readers to perceive others and the world.

Throughout the theorization of metafiction, there have been other terms that were invented to relate to experimentation and self-expression such as anti-novel, black humor, surfiction, and postmodernism. The term anti-novel did not stand the judgment of time because William Gass has remarked that most critics are far too eager to label any unusual work of fiction as an 'anti-novel' while it

---

²¹⁰ Robert Scholes *Fabulation and Metafiction* 2–3
²¹¹ William Gass "Philosophy and the Form of Fiction" 24–25
²¹² McCaffery "The Art of Metafiction" 21
²¹³ McCaffery "The Art of Metafiction" 22

is actually metafiction. But the lines do cross between the two terms, anti-novel and metafiction, as both acknowledge the process of writing fiction. The difference lies in the choice of form as "the anti-novelist indirectly criticizes past forms and suggests new perspectives on the relationship between fiction, the artist, and reality."[214] The metafictionalist, on the other hand, uses past and present information about writing, reading, and/or experience.

The term black humor, which represented a type of experimental fiction, did not survive for long either because it is a term used to express the absurdity and cruelty of the modern world in a historical perspective. The term black humor has negative connotations concerning the fears of the contemporary world after World War II without having any reference to dealing with these fears. Metafiction, on the other hand, is a more suitable term than black humor as it has a connotation of transcending fears through narrative; it indicates using fiction to explain social and historical realities.

Surfiction was another choice for experimentation as it stresses on the fictionality of reality. Raymond Federman says, "just as the surrealists called that level of man's experience that functions in the subconscious surreality, I call that level of man's activity that reveals life as a fiction surfiction."[215] But the term surfiction failed to survive because it lacked dealing with the creative linguistic elements that characterize metafiction.

Postmodernism, as a whole concept, is used to relate to reactions to modernism in philosophy, architecture, art, culture, and literature from the end of World War II until today. Postmodernism in a literary context is confused with metafiction because both refer to properties of experimentation, but literary postmodernism usually refers to experimentations that colored fiction produced especially during the 1960s and 70s and continued until the present time. What makes metafiction a more suitable term for experimentation in fiction is that metafiction is not tied to a certain period of time. Metafictional elements have appeared in literary texts for centuries. In other words, postmodernists' use of metafiction is a continuation of an already existing narcissistic trend in the novel as it began parodically in *Don Quijote* and was handed on, through eighteenth-century critical self-awareness to nineteenth-century self-mirroring.[216]

Other less important terms that refer to experimentation in fiction include, according to Patricia Waugh, antifiction, irrealism, neo-baroque fiction, and the self-begetting novel.[217] All of these terms "imply a fiction that self-consciously reflects upon its own structure as language; all offer different perspectives on the same practice."[218] The different perspectives these terms offer show the wide range of innovations that fall under the wider umbrella of postmodern literature.

In 1970, Scholes published an important article, "Metafiction" where he uses the term William Gass had come up with, metafiction, to refer to the same

---

[214] McCaffery "The Art of Metafiction" 22
[215] Raymond Federman 7
[216] Linda Hutcheon *Narcissistic Narrative* 153
[217] Patricia Waugh 13–14
[218] Waugh 14

narrative techniques he, Scholes, referred to earlier as 'fabulation.' Scholes's article "helped cement the term metafiction in the critical vocabulary."[219] Scholes in the article discusses several literary works: John Barth's *Lost in the Fun House*, W. H. Gass's *In the Heart of the Heart of the Country*, Robert Coover's *Pricksongs and Descants*, and Donald Barthleme's *City Life*. These works, according to Scholes, display characteristics of metafiction that "assault or transcend the laws of fiction."[220] The article assimilates "all the perspectives of criticism into the fictional process itself". These works are "the products of the active intelligence grappling with the problems of living and writing in the second-half of the twentieth century."[221] However, Stirling comments that Scholes did not explicitly recognize the self-conscious and self-reflexive natures of metafictional works.

Interest and praise of applying metafictional techniques in writing literature varied according to an author's point of view of metafiction. Joyce Carol Oates writes in her article "Whose Side Are You On" published in 1972:

For many years our most promising writers have lined up obediently behind Nabokov, Beckett, and Borges, to file through a doorway marked THIS WAY OUT. How eagerly they have taken their place! If they glance around at the rest of us, who are holding back, they are ready with mechanized scorn: X is too bourgeois; X is too suburban; X is not experimental; X is being read![222]

In her article, "Oates characterizes the last two decades of American fiction as an assemblage of fragments—particles-books that are self-conscious 'cities of words' and that they [American works] ricochet off one another more often than they do off reality."[223] Oates, the prolific writer, explores the fields of metafiction through her story "Plot" which is, like Barth's *Lost in the Funhouse*, a story about the process of writing itself. Oates's "Plot" has several characteristics of metafiction: despite its title, it has no defined plot which is a sign of parody, self-irony, and playfulness; it is self-conscious of the writing process; it is fiction about fiction or story about story-telling; and it does not develop in a linear fashion but relies instead on language to convey meaning. Although "Plot" is a rewriting of Barth's "Title," "Life Story," and "Autobiography" as they are stories about an author writing a story, Oates's "Plot" is an important block in the development of metafiction in that Oates allows the gnarled mirrors of "Plot" to grasp glimpses of the external world, providing a social context to the private anguish of the typical Barthian narrator. Employing her position as reader-writer, Oates uses historical events to fill in some of the blank spaces which proliferate in the desiccated universe of Barth's fabulation.[224]

In other words, Oates makes sure that her metafiction is not only playful but also includes within it the social and historical realms of the author and/or reader.

---

[219] Grant Stirling *Narrativity of Narcissism* 29
[220] Scholes "Metafiction" 107
[221] Scholes "Metafiction" 107
[222] Joyce Carol Oates "Whose Side Are You On" 63
[223] Araujo 108
[224] Araujo 113

Through works such as her critical essay "Whose Side Are You On" and her story "Plot," Oates participates in the theorization of metafiction by saying that "the choice is between the solipsism of a certain radical metafiction and a writing of compromise, choice, and intentionality, which although experimental can nevertheless engage with the other, the audience, and the world."[225] A metafictional text, for critics and readers alike, is a creative text; it uses unconventional styles of narrative in order to engage the reader more in the interpretation of the text. In other words, metafiction uses the narrative process to call attention to the fictional world and its elements: text, reader, and narrator or writer. A writer or a narrator designs his text in a creative way for a reader to draw meaning from. A writer creatively uses metafictional elements in the form of language to widen the scope of meaning and experience for the benefit of his reader.

Although the purpose of a writer's use of metafictional elements in the design of his text may not be fully acknowledged, the actual interpretation comes from the reader. The reader becomes more involved in a text with metafictional elements than with a conventional text. In the opening page of John Barth's *The Floating Opera* (1956), he says:

"It has always seemed to me in the novels that I've read now and then, that the authors are asking a great deal of their readers who start their stories furiously in the middle of things, rather than backing or sliding slowly into them. Such a plunge into someone else's life and world…has, it seems, little of pleasure in it. No, come along with me reader, and don't fear for your weak heart. Good heaven, how does one write a novel…"[226]

Barth's early interest in engaging his reader into his text supports the influence of not the experimentalists of the early 1960s upon him but of Borges' metafictional practice which is derived from Borges' engagement with *The Nights*. Likewise, Oates' metafiction is closer to the one in *The Nights* as metafiction includes readers, writers, and social and historical concerns. Metafictional elements address a reader directly to enjoy a text and be involved in the interpretation of it. Metafiction, therefore, is "an art that recognizes its own artificiality, its own systemic existence."[227] Stories within stories are representatives of Metafiction that "operates through exaggeration of the tensions and oppositions inherent in all novels: of frame and frame-break, of technique and counter-technique, of construction and deconstruction of illusion."[228] With its famous frame narrative, *The Nights* is an ancient text that remarkably has all the above mentioned characteristics of metafiction. What *The Nights*, the metafictional text, does through stories within stories is that "it forces us to examine the nature of fiction-making from new perspectives."[229] When there are layers of fictions within a work of fiction, as is the case in *The Nights*,

---

[225] Araujo 117
[226] Barth *The Floating Opera*
[227] Davidson 485
[228] Waugh 14
[229] McCaffery 34

the reader is directed toward the examination of the different forms of realities within fictions, and also toward the examination of the values of social and historical concerns of these realities.

The theorization of metafiction continues with Robert Scholes's book, *Fabulation and Metafiction* (1979), as he discusses the range of metafiction by discussing, in detail, the same four American works of fiction he dealt with in his article "Metafiction" nine years earlier. He says that there are four dimensions of fictional forms: the fiction of ideas, the fiction of form, the fiction of existence, and the fiction of essence.[230] The fiction of ideas, where Scholes gives *Pricksongs and Descants* as an example, is fiction where the essential ideas of fiction are dominating. The fiction of form, where Scholes gives *Lost in the Funhouse* as an example, is fiction that imitates other fiction. The fiction of existence, with *City Life* as an example, aims at imitating forms of the surface structure of human behavior. The fiction of essence, with *In the Heart of the Heart of the Country* as an example, deals with the deep structure of being by going beyond behavior toward ultimate values. The previously mentioned American works are chosen by Scholes, because they are, according to him, "the product of active intelligence grappling with the problems of living and writing in the second half of the twentieth century".[231] In spite of that, Scholes does not limit metafiction to a certain period but says that these four forms are present in most significant works of fiction in varied proportions.

Ihab Hassan, a university professor, critic, and a prominent figure in the field of experimentation in literature does not deal much with metafiction in particular but looks at the whole of the postmodern movement in arts in general in both of his books *Paracriticism: Seven Speculations of the Times* (1975) and *Dismemberment of Orpheus* (1982). Hassan's views on experimentation in literature are important for this debate as they offer a look at fiction as part of art, society, and cultural change. Hassan does not define what postmodernism is, or give an exact period for its start. He asserts that "the secret of innovation is motion."[232] As long as writers of fiction are moving towards innovation, they are according to Hassan on the right track. Hassan agrees with Linda Hutcheon in that experimentation in narrative (metafictional techniques are forms of experimentation) has been with us for a long time. According to Hassan, drawing a line between modernism and postmodernism is inappropriate since modernism and postmodernism do meet in movements and in works by certain authors and in certain times: "Blake, Sade, Lautreamont, Rimbaud, Mallarme, Whitman, etc....dadada, surrealism, Kafka, *Finnegans Wake*, *The Cantos*,???"[233] Hassan's tendency of not restricting the start of experimentation in fiction to the postmodernism of the 1960s and 70s has probably been a factor that more and more studies are doing just the same.

---

[230] Scholes *Fabulation and Metafiction* 108–110
[231] Scholes *Fabulation and Metafiction* 114
[232] Ihab Hassan *Paracriticism* 41
[233] Hassan *Paracriticism* 48

Unlike Robert Scholes and Ihab Hassan who appear very careful not to tie metafictional techniques in literature to a certain period of time, Patricia Waugh in her book *Metafiction: The Theory and Practice of Self-conscious Fiction* (1984), connects metafiction with postmodernism and the 1960s. She says, "Metafiction is a mode of writing within a broader cultural movement often referred to as post-modernism."[234] Postmodernism, she argues, is not easily defined as modernism[235]; postmodernism, according to her, creates a sense of alienation between writers and their societies. But Waugh asks: "How can metafiction be 'placed' within the evolution of the novel, as well as within the context of non-literary culture, and still be seen as a point of renewal rather than a sign of exhaustion?"[236] Waugh comes out of this dilemma by saying that experimental fiction has to have an audience which is self-conscious of the language of literature and its capacities. This audience, according to her, are the contemporary recipients of literature who are witnessing new developments in communication, commerce, and technologies.[237] Waugh says, "Literature…becomes a means of renewing perception by exposing and revealing the habitual and the conventional."[238] Although Waugh's book is important in the metafictional debate, the weakness in Waugh's argument in her book *Metafiction: The Theory and Practice of Self-conscious Fiction* is spotted by Ann Jefferson in her review of the book saying, "the trouble is that Waugh cannot have it both ways, and present metafiction both as an inherent characteristic of narrative fiction and as a response to the contemporary social and cultural vision."[239] In spite of the flaw in Patricia Waugh's book, it presents a good review of the various terms that reflect writers' views of constructing the world such as metapolitics, metarhetoric, metatheatre, and metafiction. "'Meta' terms, therefore, are required in order to explore the relationship between…the world of the fiction and the world outside the fiction."[240]

The establishment of metafiction as a term needed an establishment of a definition for metafiction. Although John Barth contributes a short blanket definition of metafiction as being a 'novel that imitates a novel rather than the real world,' the most widely spread definition of metafiction is by Patricia Waugh who describes metafiction as "fictional writing which self-consciously and systematically draws attention to its status as an artifact in order to pose questions about the relationship between fiction and reality."[241] Metafictional works, Waugh says, "explore a theory of writing fiction through the practice of writing fiction."[242] But providing one definition of metafiction is rather hard

---

[234] Waugh 21

[235] Waugh 10

[236] Waugh 63

[237] Waugh 64

[238] Waugh 65

[239] Ann Jefferson 574

[240] Waugh 3

[241] Waugh 2

[242] Waugh 2

since it needs to cover all characteristics and techniques of metafiction including the affinities it enjoys with other subjects and disciplines and the new terms it acquires with the passage of time.

In the second half of the 1980s, Linda Hutcheon in her book *A Poetics of Postmodernism: History, Theory, Fiction* (1988), coins a new term, historiographic metafiction, which deals with self-reflexivity which is an important characteristic of metafiction that had not been theorized until Hutcheon coined the term. Works of historiographic metafiction are well known and popular fictions with actual historic facts in fictional settings. Historiographic metafiction "provides and undermines context."[243] Historiographic metafictions, therefore, are rewritings of historical facts in new contexts using elements of metafiction such as parody and playfulness. In spite of the use of parody and playfulness, historiographic metafiction is more serious than it appears as the intersection of history and literature that historiographic metafiction implies…is a singular contribution to an effort to politicize and problematize our interpretations of the textual past. Arising out of the analysis of theorists like Hayden White and Michel Foucault, this questioning of the nature and influence of history enables, by using fiction, both a self-reflexive re-examination of historical tenets as well as a playful reconstruction of alternative historical versions which the official version has deliberately forgotten.[244]

Historiographic metafiction is, then, a rewriting of history from new perspectives. Even though it was not coined as a term until the second half of the 1980s, historiographic metafiction is a characteristic of metafiction that appears in the fictions of a number of the pioneers of metafiction such as Jorge Luis Borges, Thomas Pyncheon, and Salman Rushdie. It also appears in *The Nights* in stories about Cairo, Baghdad, Basra, Haroun Al Rasheed, etc.

The relative establishment of metafiction as a term, as a definition, and as a technique has led to studies that deal with different issues concerning metafiction or experimentation in literature. Some critics such as Larry McCaffery, a university professor and literary critic, has devoted a lot of work on metafiction. In 1976, McCaffery published an article, "The Art of Metafiction: William Gass's Willie Master's Lonesome Wife," where he looks at the nature of metafiction. He says:

"As the best metafiction does, *Willie Master's Lonesome Wife* forces us to examine the nature of fiction-making from new perspectives. If Babs (and Gass) have succeeded, our attention has been focused on the act of reading words in a way we probably have not experienced before. The steady concern with the *stuff* of fiction, words, makes Gass's work unique among metafictions which have appeared thus far."[245]

McCaffery, at the end of his article, appreciates Gass's directly addressing his reader by his closing sentence: 'YOU HAVE FALLEN INTO ART—RETURN TO LIFE' as it gives readers chances to appreciate Gass's fictional

---

[243] Hutcheon *A Poetics* 127
[244] Barry Samuel Pomeroy 4
[245] William Gass "The Art of Metafiction: Willie Master's Lonesome Wife" 34

creation as fictional. The metafictional characteristic of directly addressing the reader which Professor Larry McCaffery acknowledges as the best metafictional characteristic in a text abounds in *The Nights*.

As an example of McCaffery's interest in the development of literary theory, he published *Some Other Frequency: Interviews with Innovative American Authors* (1996). In this book, he interviews fourteen 'radically innovative' American authors in an attempt to find out what triggers innovation in each of them. MacCaffery interviewees include Lydia Davis, Richard Kostelanetz, William T. Vollmann, Mark Leyner, Gerald Vizenor, Lyn Hejinian, Ken Gangemi, Robert Kelly, Clarence Major, David Antin, and Marianne Hauser. MacCaffery says about his choice:

"the writers interviewed here are less a cohesive 'movement' sharing specific backgrounds, literary assumptions, and aesthetic goals than a kind of spiritual community of individuals bound together primarily by a shared interest in employing aesthetic innovation in their writing as a means of enlarging their readers' perceptions and injecting meaningful choices, diversity, and unprogrammable possibilities."[246]

MacCaffery's interviews offer numerous and diverse possibilities for the beginning of innovation of literature or metafiction to postmodernism and the 1960s in general.

However, MacCaffery finds a surprising result from these interviews which is a refutation of the view that experimentation in literature is antirealistic or that it represents a "retreat from reality into the endlessly (self-) reflecting 'mirror stage' of Barth's funhouse."[247] What emerges from these interviews, MacCaffery says, is "the sense that even the most radically innovative American authors retain an allegiance to realism's dictum to 'tell it like it is.'" He adds "it is the nature of the telling, as well as of the 'it,' that have been transformed as writers increasingly recognize that fiction's inability to produce truth-functions concerning our shared postmodern condition in no way precludes its ability to render 'the real life' in a realistic manner."[248] This indicates that the favored version of metafiction is the formally structured type found in *The Nights*.

The continued connecting of Metafiction with postmodernism by a number of writers and critics has led to the search for another issue concerning metafiction, which are reasons for the rise of metafiction in the sixties. Cultural effect has been strongly taken into consideration as a vital force. The reason is that metafiction, according to Grant Stirling, has many applications. In his dissertation *The Narrativity of Narcissism: Cultural Contexts of Contemporary American Metafiction* (1998), Stirling thinks that metafiction is an opposition or a reaction to modernism. Stirling says:

Although the terms of the debate surrounding the rise of metafiction and its relationship to dominant literary codes of realism and modernism is more complex than is suggested by the association of the rise of metafiction with a

---

[246] McCaffery *Some Other Frequency* 6
[247] McCaffery *Some Other Frequency* 10
[248] McCaffery *Some Other Frequency* 10

growing awareness of the degraded referential properties language, there is no doubt that this association lies at the core of critical consciousness in the mid-seventies.[249]

While Waugh, many of McCaffrey's interviewees and Stirling tie metafiction to experimentation in literature that led to the postmodernism of the end of the 1960s, Linda Hutcheon is one of the critics who think that "Self-conscious metafiction has been with us for a long time, probably since Homer and certainly since *Don Quixote* and *Tristram Shandy*."[250] Hutcheon in her discussion of postmodernism does not limit metafiction to the postmodern period. In her book *Narcissistic Narrative,* Hutcheon turns to a more important issue by seeing metafiction as a powerful tool that raises questions concerning the role of culture in the creation process of literature itself. Since the publication of *Narcissistic Narrative* in 1980, Hutcheon's views that broaden the applications of metafictional techniques beyond a certain time limit have been attracting numerous studies that are in favor of the strong influence of culture on narrative creations. Hutcheon's new coined term, historiographic metafiction, dominated the scene for a while as an explanation for the existence of metafiction beyond history. "The key to narrative development," Hutcheon asserts, "lies in the unmasking of dead literary conventions and the establishing of new literary codes."[251] Barry S. Pomeroy adds to the importance of time to fiction saying that, "Historiographic metafiction works within the dominant forms/political structures in order to overturn—by questioning the twin discourses of history and fiction—the methods/notions of veracity and authority upon which these societal structures depend."[252] In addition, historiographic metafiction, according to Mark Currie, is "epistemological: it raises issues about knowledge of the past and the bearings that narrative has on that knowledge."[253] The narrative technique of mixing history with fiction, or historiographic metafiction, is another step on the positive direction of constructing a fiction that reflects its author's views and opinions of life, reality, and truth. The presence of historiographic metafiction in *The Nights* calls for more epistemological studies of forms/political and cultural structures that have led to the finalizing of the tremendous text, *The Nights*.

To sum up this chapter and find a sense of where literary theory in general and metafiction (a component of literary theory as metafiction is techniques and structure) in particular are heading, a quick look at what critics have been saying about this literary device throughout the last six decades is appropriate. Roughly from after World War II until now, metafictional techniques still appear in works of famous writers almost all over the world. These techniques were direct developments of literary changes that started shy then took off and began to be very popular in a matter of a decade or so. "Borges, by example, taught a

---

[249] Stirling *The Narrativity of Narcissism* 61
[250] Hutcheon *A Poetics* 41
[251] Hutcheon *Narcissistic Narrative* 38
[252] Barry S. Pomeroy 267
[253] Mark Currie *Postmodern Narrative Theory* 65

generation to write stories that looked more like essays and sketches than fictional narratives. Everyone had a tale to tell. The priestly hush that attended the worship of art in the fifties was dispelled."[254]

During the 1960s, metafiction flourished and many prominent writers of fiction, such as Barth, Nabocov, McCaffery, Pynchon, Gass, and others have been drawn into its domain even though it has not been theorized as such. Fiction, according to Mark Currie who has published several books on literary criticism, has witnessed several changes during that era. It was mainly fiction about fiction. Fiction was tightly connected with the writing process itself as a means to dramatize the boundary between fiction and criticism.[255] This was performed to stress the artificiality of the so-called real world and to magnify the role of the story-teller and how he views his world. Morris Dickstein says that in the 1960s there was a 'confessional thrust' in an aim to "liberate art from a stagnant formalism and bring it closer to experience… As the 1960s unfold, the lines between different kinds of writing—and between art and life—blurred."[256] Therefore, metafiction, during that era, was seen as a linguistic construct and as part of the postmodern movement with issues and developments that tried to deal with social and cultural problems that prevailed after World War II.

During the 1970s, metafiction continued to place itself between fiction and criticism as writers have incorporated hints from the process of writing within their fiction. Metafiction has developed to display self-consciousness, self-awareness, self-knowledge, and ironic self-distance. These properties contradict most theories of postmodernism as "the liberating thrust of direct personal expression gave way to an unimaginative dependence on the writer's own story."[257] It is not only experimentation a writer is after; it is a novel way of self-expression. The close of the 1970s witnessed the production of Edward Said's book, *Orientalism* (1978) that has had a tremendous effect on literature although it is mainly about cultural and postcolonial studies. Western attitudes towards texts produced in the East, translated from Arabic, in particular, or written by Easterners living in the West have changed after Said's book. The East is not only an exotic erotic place but it is also a real world where real humans with the same concerns and worries as those of the Westerners, live. The reception and writers' reflections of works such as *The Nights* have also changed with the spread of the effect of Said's book. The 1970s also witnessed the onset of globalization as communication means helped in making Earth a small place. A work of fiction or criticism produced in a corner of the Earth is no longer confined to its place of origin; it soon travels everywhere and its effect reaches everyone.[258] Scientific developments, represented in chaos theory, have their

---

[254] Morris Dickstein 185

[255] Currie *Metafiction* 95

[256] Dickstein 185

[257] Dickstein 186

[258] See Tatsumi's "Comparative Metafiction: Somewhere between Ideology and Rhetoric" for more insights on the development of techniques of metafiction.

share in changing peoples' views of themselves and their universe. The last three points will be elaborated on as the book develops.

After the 1960s and the 1970s, the 1980s "seems to have been signaled by the consolidation of narratology…in a series of handbooks and synoptic surveys of the state of the art."[259] Linda Hutcheon, Patricia Waugh, John Barth, Ihab Hassan, Susan Sniader Lanser, and Fredrick Jameson produced publications that witnessed a return to a more historical approach that was "heavily influenced by rhetorical theories of textuality, discourse, and ideology it first came to counteract."[260] In other words, "the novel has become a philosophical novel, much better qualified than traditional discursive philosophy to address the question of the knowability of the past because it is stuck in the orbit of fiction and narrative."[261] However, Dickstein quotes Edward Said who says that literary theory for the most part isolated textuality from the circumstances, the events, the physical senses that made it possible and render it intelligible as the result of human work.[262] As a consequence of international forces such as globalization and of theorization of fiction such as the ones done by Waugh, Barth, Said, and Jameson, and as a result of the fragmented aspects of most of the cultures during the second half of the twentieth century, the flow of fiction and its theorization have been driven away from reason and logic or radical experimentation towards philosophy and appreciation of personal experience.

From another perspective, there was in the 1980s an increased interest in the metafictional technique of frame narratives as a sign of return to a more traditional form of writing fiction. In Barth's 1981 essay, "Tales within Tales within Tales," he favors frame narratives as they speak to "much ordinary experience and activity: namely, regression (or digression) and return, and theme and variation."[263] The development of the flourish of metafiction from the 1960s until the 1980s has been heading, then, to a return to a type of metafiction found in *The Nights*.

The gradual evolution of narrative during the 1990s, driven by the aforementioned forces, has led to further change as fiction continued to struggle with language in an attempt to find exact words, phrases, and expressions to represent cultural and social issues. Christy Burns in her article, "Rethinking modernism after the 1990s," says:

"In an attempt to find clear representations, the politics of representation, the politics of style, questions about sexuality, the emergence of queer theory and gender studies, and a full embrace of (post)colonial critique—all served to change the face of modernism, throwing previously held beliefs and narratives into doubt."[264]

---

[259] Brian McHale 4

[260] Dickstein xi–xii

[261] Currie *Postmodern Narrative Theory* 65

[262] Dickstein xi

[263] Barth *Friday Book* 237

[264] Christy Burns 470

In spite of that, and as a form of reality, fiction during the new millennium has continued to celebrate authorial self-consciousness in addition to reflecting historical and political realities of the period. Major events such as the 9/11 attacks on the most powerful Western nation have been included, explicitly or implicitly, in almost all fictions of the period creating metafictional texts. Metafictional Narrative has become part of the consciousness of the contemporary interpretation of life and living.

This, indeed, is not everything there is concerning the origin of metafiction and its development. Consequently, the origin of metafiction deserves another attempt for explanation by examining *The Nights* with its obvious characteristics of metafiction. That will be discussed in the following chapter.

Chapter III
Naguib Mahfouz's Arabian Nights and Days and Metafiction

Metafiction and "the art of nights" are the main interests of this book. To explore these subjects further, this chapter deals with another contemporary metafictional work that is also part of "the art of nights." Naguib Mahfouz, the Nobel Prize winner and well-known Egyptian author, published in 1979, in Arabic, his novel, ليالي ألف ليلة *Layali Alf Laylah* which was translated into English by Denys Johnson-Davies and published in 1995 under the title *Arabian Nights and Days*.[265] This chapter gives a briefing about Mahfouz's literary trajectory then moves to his novel *Arabian Nights and Days* to explain its affinities with the original, *The Nights*, and with metafiction.

Naguib Mahfouz was born in 1911 just before World War I, but it was not this war that affected him tremendously; it was the 1919 revolution against English occupation of Egypt. Mahfouz was about seven years old when he witnessed English soldiers fire at demonstrators killing men and women. Witnessing these incidents awakened young Mahfouz's political awareness and played a role in his direction towards history in his early fiction then to social reform and liberal principles in his later fiction.[266]

Mahfouz started writing during the early 1930s before graduating from Cairo University majoring in philosophy in 1934. The reason he chose philosophy was that he had "a desire to know the secret of the universe and the mysteries of existence."[267] A couple of years after his graduation, he decided to commit himself to writing fiction where he could freely express his philosophical thoughts. At the same time, he continued to work, for a living, as a civil servant until his retirement in 1972. His job[268], Mahfouz says: "gave me the opportunity

---

[265] I chose Mahfouz's *Arabian Nights and Days* as a contemporary reworking of the original, *The Nights*, instead of other Arab works such as Al-Hakim's, Husein, or Ba-Kathir's because Mahfouz's *Nights* was produced and translated into English after the 1960s flood of experimentation in fiction.

[266] El-Enany *Naguib Mahfouz: His Life and Time* 3

[267] Al-Ghitani 15

[268] There is a similarity between Mahfouz and Barth in that they both acknowledge their first jobs as helpful in enriching their experiences. Barth was working in filing books in a university library, and Mahfouz was working as a civil servant meeting people with real life situations.

to become acquainted with numerous human situations and types that had an impact on what I wrote. It also provided me with the wherewithal to deal with life."[269] He never stopped writing and continued to produce until near his death in 2006. At first, Mahfouz started by writing articles and short stories, but his greatest achievements were novels. Stretching over the span of over seventy years, Mahfouz's works include thirty-four novels, about 350 short stories, five plays, and a number of movie scripts and countless essays.

When reviewing Mahfouz's literary trajectory, two major shifts can be seen. He started with realism during the 1930s, 40s, and up until the late 50s. Then he moved to modernism during the rest of the 1950s, 60s, and early 70s. From the 1970s until the end of his writing career around 2004, he shifted in some of his major works to postmodernism and metafiction. During the 1930s and up until the middle of the 1940s, the young Naguib Mahfouz was interested in history as a means to explain human behavior. Realism in fiction was his first choice of expression. He read Tolstoy's *War and Peace* and Dostoevsky's *Crime and Punishment*. He read some works of Chekhov, Maupassant, Kafka, Proust, Joyce, Eugene O'Neil, Ibsen, Strindberg and Shakespeare.[270] "All of them," he says, "contributed to shaping me as a writer. And when I wrote, I did not fall under the influence of any one in particular. I was not dazzled by modern technical developments. Imagine if I'd been influenced by Joyce, and tried to follow the stream-of-consciousness path! I read *Ulysses* in the mid-thirties. However, when I started writing, I jettisoned all that and went down the realist path."[271]

Mahfouz started the realist path to write his first novels: مصر القديمة *Old Egypt* (1932); همس الجنون *Whisper of Madness* (1938); عبث الأقدار(1939) translated into English as *Khufu's Wisdom* in 2004; رادوبيس (1943) translated into English as *Rhadopis of Nubia* in 2005; and كفاح طيبة(1944), translated into English as *Thebes at War* in 2004. Most of these works, especially the last three, were historical novels, written as part of a large never completed project of about 40 novels intended to cover the whole history of Egypt.

Beginning from 1945 and after the third historical novel, Mahfouz lost interest in the past and moved to the present. Mahfouz says, "History was dead. What would bring it back to life? What was the cause of its death? I didn't know."[272] Mahfouz, instead, became interested in the effect of social change and social justice on individual behavior. Mahfouz's narrative style during his historical then social periods, therefore, reveals affinities with the Western form of the novel during the realist and early modernist periods. However, some of these novels, especially *Cairo Modern* in the depiction of Mahgoub, one of its main characters, reveals Mahfouz's interest in personal actions. Instead of blaming society or religion for the faults of man, it is man himself, the building block of society, who is to be blamed for his own faults. Mahfouz's early

---

[269] Al-Ghitani 38

[270] Al-Ghitani 87

[271] Al-Ghitani 87

[272] Al-Ghitani 89

recognition of the consequences of personal actions, therefore, has contributed, in one way or another, to the appearance of small narrative units incorporated into larger bodies of work.

Still realistic, Mahfouz's work in the second half of the 1950s deals with the recent history of Egypt, but he mixes that with social preoccupation and produced one of his major works: الثلاثية/*The Cairo Trilogy*. This trilogy is a social and historical work that consists of three novels carrying names of streets in Cairo, بين القصرين (1956,) translated as *Palace Walk* in 1989; قصر الشوق (1957,) translated as *Palace of Desire* in 1991; and السكرية (1957,) translated as *Sugar Street* in 1992. This three-part epic follows Al-Sayyed Ahmad Abd Al Jawwad and his family over three generations stretching from the 1910s to the 1950s when the monarchy in Egypt was overthrown. Highly praised by Western criticism, this trilogy represents the height of Mahfouz's realist period. The Trilogy is also "a study of the intimate relationships between men and women, as well as an account of the search for faith."[273] Mahfouz was accordingly called 'The Balzac of Egypt.' Fatma Moussa-Mahmoud, in her book *The Arabic Novel in Egypt*, says:

"The realistic tradition in the Arabic novel was firmly established by the end of the fifties. Naguib Mahfouz probably contributed more than any Arab novelist towards establishing this tradition. His *Trilogy* marks the peak of this achievement, a necessary stage for him and for other writers to proceed with new experiments."[274]

However, inside this realistic trilogy there is what Rasheed El-Enany calls aspect of the relationship between time and man, namely the relationship between past and present. This relationship in Mahfouz's trilogy, according to El-Enany, "transfers us from the realm of metaphysical time to that of value-impregnated time,"[275] which means that what man does with time is crucial to him and to society. Mahfouz's philosophical views in his early fiction has led him away from reality and into newly explored realms of fiction. Interestingly, therefore, the trilogy also marks the end of the realist period as "the moment Mahfouz felt that he had mastered the techniques of realism and exhausted their potential, that is by writing *The Trilogy*, he was to cast realism behind him and plunge into the deep and turbulent waters of modernism."[276]

In addition, Mahfouz was aware of the controversy regarding the limited ability of the realist mode of writing to express the life of uncertainty after World War II. He says, "I wrote in the realist style and at the very same time I was reading the most savage attacks on realism."[277] Mahfouz, therefore, has always been a sensitive writer who knew his craft well, and who knew the developments it had been taking worldwide. *The Trilogy*, according to Mahfouz himself, comes from a classic age, ends deep in a romantic age, and is headed toward an analytic

---

[273] Edward Said "Cruelty of Memory"
[274] Fatma Moussa-Mahmoud 63
[275] El-Enany *His Life and Time* 75
[276] El-Enany *The Pursuit of Meaning* 19
[277] Al-Ghitani 87

age. In it the East meets the West, but not through journeys such as those undertaken by Tawfiq al-Hakim or Yahya Hakki or al-Tayyib Salih. It represents the person who found the West while in the East, the manifestations of civilization coming to his doorsteps, and who had no choice but to interpret these changes in the soul, the spirit, and the mind.[278]

It is interesting to note, though, that originally Mahfouz had written the 1500-page *Trilogy* to be published as one whole work and not as three separate novels. In his notes to *Naguib Mahfouz: The Pursuit of Meaning*, Rasheed El-Enany says:

"Originally it [*The Trilogy*] was written as one piece with the title 'Bayn al-Qasrayn,' but Mahfouz's publisher rejected it on account of its excessive length. However, when what later came to be known as the first part of *The Trilogy* was successfully serialized in the then literary magazine *Al-Risala al-Jadida*...the publisher changed his mind and suggested to Mahfouz that he should divide the book into three parts with different titles."[279]

Accordingly, the analytic age Mahfouz was aiming at when he gave *The Trilogy* its unified yet fragmented structure was an early intentional step towards innovation in writing fiction. That innovative step (that carries metafictional tendencies due to its three-part structure) went unnoticed because of the wrong decision of the publisher that led to the division of the novel into three separate works.

After the trilogy, Mahfouz's narrative style reveals changes that are similar to changes other authors around the world have been taking. Critics of Mahfouz's works such as Sasson Somekh, in his book *The Changing Rhythm: A Study of Najib Mahfuz's Novels*, emphasizes the shift in his literature after World War II as neo-realistic or modern tendencies because the novels still depict the Egyptian life-style.[280] However, changes in Mahfouz's style at that period appear more subtle. After World War II, the value of expressing personal experience began to spread and take precedence in works of authors such as Jorge Luis Borges, John Barth, and many others. In the Arab World, it was Mahfouz who "transcends the traditional 18th and 19th century prose novel form of single narrative perspective and delves deeply into the social consciousness represented in his works through his use of fragmented character narratives."[281] In 1959 modernist techniques such as symbolism, recurrent motifs, and stream of consciousness techniques started to appear strongly in his fiction beginning from 1959. This period is the prolific period that started with the publication of أولاد حارتنا *Awlaad Haratina* in a serial form in Al-Ahram newspaper, but the novel was not published whole until 1967 in Beirut. This novel was later translated into English in 1981 under the title, *Children of Gebelawi*, and in 1996 under the title, *Children of the Alley*. *Awlaad Haratina* stirred a lot of controversy in the religious circles in the Arab world because of its content that deals with man's plight in search of truth through

---

[278] Al-Ghitani 104
[279] El-Enany *The Pursuit of Meaning* 225–226. Al-Ghitani 96–97
[280] Sasson Somekh 36
[281] Winter 4

belief or religion. To most people, religions are grand narratives that are not supposed to be touched, and Mahfouz has touched the untouchable. His thematic manifestations can be seen now as metafictional, since metafictional works deconstruct grand narratives. Unfortunately, this novel has led to the assassination attempt against Mahfouz in 1994. Internationally and because of its subject matter, this novel was thought to have paved the way for Salman Rushdie's *Satanic Verses*, another novel touching the untouchable.

Although controversial, the universality of themes in *Awlaad Haratina* and in many of Mahfouz's works has led to his receiving the Nobel Prize for Literature in 1988. Sture Allen, of the Swedish Academy, attributes to Mahfouz's work "the forming of an Arabian narrative art that applies to all mankind."[282] This kind of narrative art has been in the Arab World for centuries in *The Nights*. This classic has been a source of joy and inspiration for all readers because of its special narrative style and universal themes.

From the end of the 1950s until the middle of the 1970s, Mahfouz's style was modernist. He published اللص والكلاب (1961,) translated into English as *The Thief and the Dogs* in 1984. This novel was a success when it first appeared for two reasons. First, Mahfouz heavily uses the stream of consciousness technique, a newly explored narrative technique in fiction written in Arabic. The author has almost a sole protagonist, and other characters in the novel appear through the consciousness of the main protagonist in order to expose his inner conflicts in trying to deal with personal behavior, society, religion, and life in general. Second, Mahfouz exposes some weaknesses in the political system of Egypt in the beginning of the 1960s. Mahfouz's protagonist is a Marxist who plans revenge after he gets out of prison. According to El-Enany in his book, *Naguib Mahfouz: His Life and Time, The Thief and the Dogs*, the author's first link in the chain dealing directly with the shortcomings of the 1952 revolution, is about betrayal, mainly the betrayal of revolutionary ideas once power, with the privileges that come with it, is achieved.[283]

Mahfouz's work always shows his occupation with literary developments and with changes in his society and their effect on the individual. Therefore, not only his themes but also his writing style reflect these changes and the turbulences they cause in the country.

During the 1960s, Mahfouz published several modernist novels. In 1962, he published السمان والخريف, translated into *Autumn Quail* in 1985, where he "pursues his examination of the relationship between the individual and authority, and again the theme of the corrupting influence of power over the one-time revolutionary."[284] The same political atmosphere prevails in his short story collections, دنيا الله (1962,) translated as *God's World* and زعبلاوي (1963,) translated as *Zaabalawi* as well as in his novel, الطريق (1964,) translated as *The Search* in 1987. الشحاذ (1965,) translated as *The Beggar* in 1986, and ثرثرة فوق النيل (1966,) translated into English as *A drift on the Nile* in 1993 are all, in general,

---

[282] Winter 3

[283] El-Enany *His Life and Time* 94

[284] El-Enany *His Life and Time* 97

modernist novels with a political taste. In 1967, Mahfouz published his novel, ميرامار, translated into English as *Miramar* in 1978. It is a political novel with four first-person narrators representing different political views, and has a trace of fragmentation in its narrative style. In 1969, Mahfouz's collection of short stories, *Khammarat Al Qitt Al Aswad (The Tavern of the Black Cat)*, appeared. One of its stories, "Shahrazad," marks Mahfouz's first explicit engagement with *The Nights*. Specifically in this short story, Mahfouz recognizes the metafictional technique of interruption in the original, *The Nights*, by constructing his story around a woman named Shahrazad who tells a journalist her problems/stories through several interrupted telephone calls. The calls "serve to create suspense and anticipation at the other end with the male listener."[285]

From the beginning of the 1970s until the end of his literary career in 2005, some of Mahfouz's major works show a shift to a new direction, a movement from modernism to postmodernism and metafiction. His movement coincides, to a large degree, with the movement of narrative style in the West in the same direction though a little late in time. Edward Said recognizes shifts in Mahfouz's style of writing by saying:

"Mahfouz has been characterized since he became a recognized world celebrity as either a social realist in the mode of Balzac, Galsworthy, and Zola or a fabulist straight out of the Arabian Nights… It is closer to the truth to see him…as providing in his novels a kind of history of the novel form, from historical fiction to the romance, saga, and picaresque tale, followed by work in realist, modernist, naturalist, symbolist, and absurdist modes."[286]

Rasheed El-Enany in both his books, *Naguib Mahfouz: The Pursuit of Meaning* and *Naguib Mahfouz: His Life and Times*[287] recognizes the shift in Mahfouz's style away from modernism and calls Mahfouz's novels that best display this style the 'episodic novels' due to fragmentations in their structure. El-Enany locates the origin of such style in ancient and Arab works as *Ayyam al-'arab* (the battle days of the Arabs), *Kalila wa Dimna* (adopted by the Arabs from Indian and Persian origins), *Maqamat al-Hamadhani*, *The Nights*, *Sirat Bani Hilal*, and *Sirat 'Antar*. These works, according to El-Enany, have "semi-independent episodes,"[288] held together either by a frame narrative as in the cases of *Kalila wa Dimna* and *The Nights*, or by having the same central figure or hero as in the cases of *Al Maqamat* and the Siras. Each of these episodic narratives or fragments "is called a *hikaya* (tale),"[289] and it forms an independent unit of discourse. El-Enany states:

"Evidently none of these Arabic narrative forms conforms to the traditional Western definition of plot as laid down by Aristotle (384–322 BC) in his *Poetics*,

---

[285] Ghazoul *Nocturnal Poetics* 137

[286] Said "Cruelty of Memory" nil

[287] I rely fairly heavily on both of El-Enany's books because they provide a thorough study of Mahfouz's changes in narrative style and the appearance of fragmentation in his fiction

[288] El-Enany *His Life and Times* 108

[289] El-Enany *His Life and Times* 111

and which has largely governed the structure of the Western novel since its evolution and until fairly recently."[290]

El-Enany acknowledges the fact that when Mahfouz started writing fiction, he followed realist then modernist Western examples. However, when recognizing what he calls the 'episodic novels' of Mahfouz, El-Enany does not refer them to metafiction. Mahfouz, according to El-Enany, was to create an episodic mold of his own and pour into it some of the most astounding achievements of his creative imagination, such as *The Harafish* and *Arabian Nights and Days*. It was from the early 1970s onwards that Mahfouz tended increasingly to express himself in the episodic mode though not to the exclusion of the familiar Western form, which he continued to use sporadically.[291]

On another occasion, when discussing Mahfouz's *Al Harafish* as an episodic novel, El-Enany says:

"In using the word *harafish* and making them the protagonists of his novel, which is written in the episodic form, indigenous to popular Arabic literature, Mahfouz was in fact reviving, modernizing, and endowing with a new vision a well-established popular, narrative form whose tradition includes parts of *The Arabian Nights* and the famous popular *siras* (heroic exploits) of *'Antara b. Shadad, Hamzat al-'Arab* and *Zahir Baybars*, to name some of the better-known examples."[292]

El-Enany, nevertheless, does not make clear the link between Mahfouz's creative revival of the traditional Arabic narrative form and the movement, in the West, in the same direction. Roughly, from the end of World War II, a large number of Western literary writers have abandoned the familiar modern narrative style in favor of a metafictional style. As it is well known, the metafictional narrative style is represented in some of its aspects by the inclusion of a reference to the process of narration within a narrative creating a frame narrative with smaller units of narrative within it. The style of Mahfouz, in some of his best novels beginning from the early 1970s, is a metafictional style that El-Enany calls episodic.

In addition, it is well-documented that Mahfouz had been following the development of the novel in the West.[293] When the Western novelists used

---

[290] El-Enany *His Life and Times*108–09

[291] El-Enany *His Life and Times* 109–110

[292] El-Enany *The Pursuit of Meaning* 240. El-Enany does not recognize the distinctively fragmented narrative style in Al Qur'an recognized by Mahfouz in his late years. Mahfouz says, "The stories told in the Qur'an follow the most modern principles of novel writing. They do not begin, like nineteenth-century novels, by setting the stage for the drama, the build up toward a climax, before reaching a resolution in the last pages. They are more like twentieth-century literary experiments, in which events do not follow a monotonous, diachronic sequence but move according to dramatic requirements, which dictate where the different parts of the story are located. In modern European novel writing, this represented a revolution, as can be seen in the works of Joyce or Proust" (Salmawy Naguib Mahfouz at Sidi Gaber 66).

[293] Al-Ghitani *The Mahfouz Dialogs* 86–87; El-Enany *Naguib Mahfouz: The Pursuit of Meaning* 11–12; and El-Enany *Naguib Mahfouz: His Life and Times* 17–18

referentiality, self-reflexivity, and fragmentation, Mahfouz followed. However, Mahfouz has a greater advantage over Western writers to stabilize the newly adopted fragmented narrative style in *The Nights*. This is because Mahfouz is a native speaker of Arabic and a part of the culture that sometimes produced that style and sometimes received and nurtured it. The superiority of Mahfouz in this regard will be acknowledged when discussing novels from his metafictional period.

There are several novels by Mahfouz that show techniques of metafiction. El-Enany refers to these novels as episodic. They are: المرايا *Mirrors* (1972), حكايات حارتنا *Fountain and Tomb* (1975), الحرافيش *Al Harafish* (1977), and ليالي ألف ليلة *Arabian Nights and Days* (1979). These works display self-reflexivity as there is insistence on story-telling and on their fictional nature. They also show fragmentation as each of them is divided into several narrative units. Self-reflexivity and fragmentation are characteristics of metafiction. Before going on to discuss the first three novels briefly and the fourth in detail, it is interesting to say that El-Enany in *Naguib Mahfouz: The Pursuit of Meaning* locates the origin of Mahfouz's shift in narrative style in his 1959 admired work, *Children of Gebelawi*. El-Enany says:

"The episodic quality of *Children of Gebelawi* was nevertheless accidental rather than intentional; that is to say it was dictated by dint of its being a religio-historical allegory meant to parallel certain 'episodes' in human history. It would therefore be correct *not* to regard it as the true beginning of the author's episodic phase."[294]

I believe, as I stated before, that the first glimpse of a change in narrative style to fragmentation that El-Enany calls episodic goes back even farther; it goes back to *The Trilogy* in its original presentation before it was divided into three separate novels. What is important to the argument of this book from this is that in 1952, the date Mahfouz finished *The Trilogy*, no practice of metafiction had been recognized. On the other hand, the date of the first appearance of *Children of Gebelawi* 1959, roughly coincides with the beginning of the spread of metafictional techniques in literature in the West.

Thirteen years after *Children of Gebelawi*, Mahfouz published المرايا *Almaraya*, translated into English under the title *Mirrors* in 1977. The metafictionality of this novel is clear as it draws attention to its fictionality. It has no plot, no beginning or closure, and it has a fragmented nature as it is composed of fifty-five-character sketches united only by an omnipresent extradiegetic narrator who sometimes turns into an intradiegetic narrator when he mentions his own interactions with his characters. In addition, the novel has no central protagonist other than its narrator. This narrator makes a cross reference between sketches when a common incident or narrative is shared. According to El-Enany, "The book is a heap of images, broken in the flux of time, each a fragment of human flotsam carried forward by the eternal current. Perhaps in the very fragmentariness of the novel is its unity."[295] From 1972, then,

---

[294] El-Enany *The Pursuit of Meaning* 129
[295] El-Enany *His Life and Times* 104

Mahfouz has enriched the trajectory of contemporary literary theory with metafictional novels that carry his imprints.

In 1975, Mahfouz published حكايات حارتنا *Hikayat Haratina*, translated into English as *Fountain and Tomb*. This novel is also composed of seventy-eight narrative units and it seems to be a continuation of *Mirrors*. *Fountain and Tomb*, according to El-Enany, "carries on from where *Mirrors* broke off: the journey into the narrator's childhood continues—the narrator here not distinguished from Mahfouz who has acknowledged that the work reflects his own childhood."[296] Nevertheless, it is more than that. In spite of its stylistic and thematic connections with *Mirrors*, this novel is different as it is more metafictional than *Mirrors*. Mahfouz himself felt that it was different. He says, "The sole literary work I have written that is unlike anything else I have read and that I cannot place within any particular school is *Fountain and Tomb*."[297] This is probably because of several reasons. First, the work openly stresses the act of narration beginning from its title as the Arabic title *Hikayat Haratina* literarily translates into *Tales of Our Alley*. Second, the novel mixes fact with fiction, reality with irreality, actual life experiences Mahfouz had witnessed with the fictional worlds he had formed from these real events. Third, Mahfouz knew that *Fountain and Tomb* which is composed of 78 *Hikaya* or tale contains the nuclei of all his written and even not yet written novels. The *Hara* (alley), the setting; the mysterious takiyah or monastery with its mysterious occupants and supposed leader and quiet garden; the cemetery; Sa'ad Zaghloul, the 1919 revolution and Egyptian nationalism; the blind huge beggar; demonstrations against the British; gangs and gang leaders; intimate relationships; atheism and monotheism; superstition and belief in jinn; young women, old women, beautiful women, strong women, and violent women; dominating men and dominated men; corruption, stealing, and treachery etc. are all there. *Fountain and Tomb*, therefore, is self-reflexive of almost all of Mahfouz's work, and self-reflexivity is a metafictional characteristic.

In his next metafictional novel, الحرافيش *The Harafish* (1977,) Mahfouz opens up to explore the whole human existence through magnifying the absurdity of some human behavior. الحرافيش *The Harafish* is composed of ten relatively long independent narratives with historical perspectives. Because the novel follows sixteen generations of the family of Ashur Al-Naji, this novel has been referred to as an epic. There is some resemblance between this novel and *Children of Gebelawi*, the first indication of change of style towards metafiction. Both novels are historical and they are both set in the *Hara* within the Cairo district, etc. However, *The Harafish* is metafictional in that its setting is not named, its temporal grounds are not defined, and it is clearly structured in ten separate narrative units. El-Enany says: "Rather than trying to interpret existing myths in terms of reality as he [Mahfouz] did in *Children of Gebelawi*, the author here condenses total reality into a tailor-made myth of his own creation."[298]

---

[296] El-Enany *His Life and Times* 111

[297] Al-Ghitani 100

[298] El-Enany *The Pursuit of Meaning* 145

In 1979, ليالي ألف ليلة *Arabian Nights and Days*, another metafictional novel by Mahfouz was published:

It is *Arabian Nights and Days* that will no doubt be remembered as his last major work. Together with *Harafish*, it represents the peak of his episodic period. Rather than create his own myth to portray his vision of the human condition…he chooses to adopt for the same purpose one of the most imaginative products of the human mind [*The Nights*].[299]

The reason is that while *The Nights* is the literary expression of its time[300], *Arabian Nights and Days* is the literary expression of Mahfouz's time even though it is set in the past. Speaking about the setting of *Arabian Nights and Days* Mahfouz says: "Imitating the past is like imitating the present: both are a form of captivity. What matters is to look for what is in harmony with your identity."[301] Mahfouz has created his own reading of the closer of the original classic in order to give his views concerning the identity of Egypt in the grip of contemporary upheaval. *Arabian Nights and Days*, therefore, represents a different world with different character roles and identities.

Of all Mahfouz's metafictional novels, choosing this one to be analyzed in this book is intentionally done for several reasons. First, Mahfouz's *Arabian Nights and Days* displays self-reflexivity as it draws attention to its fictional nature. It is in fact generated from the fictional classic, *The Nights; Arabian Nights and Days*, therefore, inherits almost all the metafictional techniques of the original. Second, *Arabian Nights and Days* is a contemporary metafictional work written by a native speaker of Arabic, the language of the original, *The Nights*, after experimentation in writing fiction boomed during the 1960s and 70s. Third and most important, *Arabian Nights and Days* is a text that has influenced the metafictionist John Barth in his depiction of the original, *The Nights,* as nowhere in *The Nights* the state of Shahrazad and how she feels at the end of these nights are included. Barth's *Ten Nights* includes a hint on how Shahrazad feels about her relationship with Shahrayar.[302] Since Mahfouz's *Arabian Nights and Days* explicitly deals with this relationship of how Shahrazad is unhappy at the end of the thousand and one nights of story-telling, this particular point is the proof that Mafouz's *Arabian Nights and Days*, translated and published in the West a decade before Barth's *Ten Nights*, is an active fiction that has affected the development of metafiction internationally through affecting Barth, one of the prominent figures in the metafictional debate. In addition, *Arabian Nights and Days* deals with the political and social situation of contemporary Egypt (although figuratively), and Barth's *Ten Nights* revolves around the political and social situation of the USA following the 9/11, 2001 ordeal. The above points, which will be thoroughly discussed in this chapter, form the purpose behind the inclusion of *Arabian Nights and Days* in this book.

---

[299] El-Enany *His life and Times* 131

[300] Ghazoul 54

[301] Al-Ghitani 107

[302] See above pp. 148–50.

To begin analyzing Mahfouz's work, it is sufficient to say that the entire text of *Arabian Nights and Days* is generated from the original, *The Nights*, as the end of the original classic is the beginning of *Arabian Nights and Days*.

Following the dawn prayer, with clouds of darkness defying the vigorous thrust of light, the vizier Dandan was called to a meeting with the sultan Shahriyar. Dandan's composure vanished. The heart of a father quaked within him as, putting on his clothes, he mumbled, "Now the outcome will be resolved—your fate, Shahrazad... Three years he had spent between fear and hope, between death and expectations; three years spent in the telling of stories; and thanks to those stories, Shahrazad's life span had been extended. Yet, like everything, the stories had come to an end, had ended yesterday. So what fate was lying in wait for you, O beloved daughter of mine?"[303]

The above quotation is a unit of discourse that brings to the mind of a reader the whole of *The Nights* as a text. That text serves as the matrix that *Arabian Nights and Days* is built upon. It is already established in Chapter II that *The Nights* is metafictional as it is a narrative about the act of narration or storytelling. Accordingly, *Arabian Nights and Days* inherits almost all narrative qualities in the original *The Nights*, including metafictionality, which becomes a metafictional matrix for *Arabian Nights and Days*. In order to qualify fully as matrix, Ferial Ghazoul says:

"The Matrix should be in the center of the whole text and not simply of the plot. It has to justify the text as it stands with its redundancies, contradictions, and digressions... It is more than the central theme of the text, for it is both the source and the formula, the stimulus and the regulator."[304]

The Nights justifies the very creation of *Arabian Nights and Days* as the latter states clearly that it is initiated after the three-year span of the original *Nights*. Not only that but the original frame story of Shahrayar and Shahrazad appears at the beginning of *Arabian Nights and Days* and also in many instances in the body of the novel, commenting on the act of narration or playing part on the narration. For instance, when Shahrayar returns from one of his night walks in his city he exchanges a conversation with Shahrazad:

"Last night," he said, "in my wandering I lit upon a story that was like one of yours, Shahrazad."

Despite her hidden sorrow, she said smiling, "The fact that stories repeat themselves is an indication of their truth Your Majesty."[305]

Mahfouz here is not only commenting on the structure of the original classic but he is also innovating a new metafictional text through self-consciously examining the structure of the original. Mahfouz's purpose is to "explore the possible fictionality of the world outside the literary fictional text."[306] The contemporary real world of Mahfouz is absurd to the point of being closer to fiction than to reality. It is not in the scope of this book to differentiate between

---

[303] Mahfouz *Arabian Nights and Days* 1
[304] Ghazoul *Structural Analysis* 51
[305] *Arabian Nights and Days* 98
[306] Waugh 2

the ontological status of Mahfouz's creation and that of the original, but the realm of psychoanalysis might help in shedding some light on the relationship between the two texts. In the major portion of *The Nights*, the analyst is Shahrazad and her stories, and the analysand is Shahrayar and his plight. That major portion, Shahrazad's stories, becomes a narcissistic narrative that exceeds the plight of Shahrayar in size and significance.[307] In Mahfouz's novel, the whole of *Arabian Nights and Days* is the analyst and the analysand is *The Nights*. However, the original classic is a formidable book within the book of *Arabian Nights and Days*; i.e. it comes to the mind of the reader as soon as s/he reads few pages from Mahfouz's *Arabian Nights and Days*. It is apparent, though, that Mahfouz's novel is condensed in form, but this appearance is misleading as it can be challenged by the relatively hidden presence of *The Nights* inside Mahfouz's novel. *Arabian Nights and Days* can be expanded systematically by using psychoanalysis and object-relation theory creating an even bigger metafictional narcissistic narrative than the one Shahrazad's stories has created in relation to the plight of Shahrayar.[308] When looking at John Barth's previously discussed novel, *Ten Nights and a Night: Eleven Stories*, one finds that its metafictionality resembles the Russian Formalist notion of defamiliarization; plot manipulations such as repetition, mirroring, fragmentation, the violation of chronological order, the expansion or contraction of duration of events, or the violation of the logical order of casual relationships between plot elements are most often interpreted as foregrounding the artificial and constructed nature of narrative.[309]

Arabian Nights and Days, on the other hand, expands the critical significance of metafiction beyond the simpler formalist notion of defamiliarization and into the connection between narcissism and metafiction. The connection between narcissism and metafiction is achieved, according to Stirling, by illustrating how metafiction can emerge as a potent means of cultural contestation in which the narrative strategies of metafictional texts operate to assert dissident cultural values. In particular, the elements of aggression and idealization that define narcissism in object-relation theory can be transposed into a critical typology that concisely expresses the primary narrative impulses that metafictional texts tend to erect within their own narrative matrices.[310]

In the relationship of *Arabian Nights and Days* to *The Nights*, the case of narcissism is the idealizing transference where "the analyst is invested with all the perfection of the idealized parent imago."[311] The condensed novel of Mahfouz is cleverly and economically structured to invest almost all narrative properties of its idealized parent, *The Nights*, in order to be a critique of

---

[307] See above, pp. 67–71.

[308] See above, pp. 67–71

[309] Stirling "Neurotic Narrative" 4

[310] Stirling "Neurotic Narrative" 2

[311] Stirling "Neurotic Narrative" 4

contemporary culture. Because he is an Easterner and native speaker of Arabic, Mahfouz, in his treatment of *The Nights*, did not have to deal with the Self and the Other as did Barth in *Ten Nights*.[312] However, Mahfouz takes a route more complex than that of Barth by using the most intricate of metafictional techniques of structure to deliver his messages.

Although closely related, the compacted structure of *Arabian Nights and Days* is completely different from the structure of the original classic; Mahfouz's novel lacks suspense, represented in the division into nights, which is considered one of the most important narrative techniques in *The Nights*. Because of its structure, *The Nights* is "a perpetual narrative."[313] This timeless narrative, because of the idealization transference explained above, becomes the matrix story for Mahfouz's novel. *Arabian Nights and Days*, consequently, still carries the ironical suspense present in *The Nights* even though Mahfouz's work lacks suspense highlighted in *The Nights* by the division into night. In *Arabian Nights and Days*, Shahrazad does not refrain from the act of narration when morning arrives and leaves her listeners suspended for the conclusion of a story. Yet, the suspension is still there in *Arabian Nights and Days* first because the astonishing original story is the matrix for Mahfouz's contemporary story. Second, using this matrix creates further astonishment that creates a form of suspense in waiting for the end of the novel to find out the fate of Shahrayar, not Shahrazad, in *Arabian Nights and Days*. In spite of its condensed size, *Arabian Nights and Days* is thematically able to incorporate the huge construct of *The Nights*. This situation sets the stage for metafictional irony as "if something astonishing is produced [*The Nights* in this case] and something more astonishing promised [*Arabian Nights and Days*], there is interest and consequently hope."[314] The relationship between the two texts, in size and in significance, creates metafictional irony.

From another point of view concerning metafictional irony, *The Nights* is the matrix and point of reference for *Arabian Nights and Days*, yet Mahfouz's work conveys meaning different from the meanings in *The Nights*. Ferial Ghazoul says, "Irony is, inevitably, a secondary development and can only be grasped through its emulation and distance from that which is being ironized."[315] *Arabian Nights and Days*, therefore, holds the whole load of the narrative ground of *The Nights*, and it is rooted in the virtue of the great classic. Yet it is, ironically, different from it in several ways.

First, the compilers of *The Nights* are not known[316] while *Arabian Nights and Days* has an author, Naguib Mahfouz. Mahfouz is a well know modern literary figure:

---

[312] See above, p. 138.

[313] Ghazoul, *A Structural Analysis* 153

[314] Roy P Mottahedeh 31

[315] Ghazoul *Structural Analysis* 69

[316] "A text without an author, issuing from the popular imagination, and which has taken its present shape through crystallization, cannot be explained in terms of the author's personality or historical conditions. No writer can take the credit or the blame for *The*

"He has been credited with inventing the modern Arab novel. The Dickensian realism and the Dickensian pathos of his literary recreation of Cairo have recommended him to non-Islamic readers in the West. But as the most recent work of his to be translated shows [*Arabian Nights and Days*], the mosaic-like depiction of urban reality in his novels reflects, from time to time, a spiritual light that issues from his own profound religious discipline. Thus Mahfouz speaks to his condition, to Egypt's—in the grip of murderous forces—and to our own…after reading *Arabian Nights and Days*, one can't but see it as an act of one who understands what he has written."[317]

This difference between *The Nights* and *Arabian Nights and Days* works to the favor of Mahfouz's work when it comes to metafictionality. Mahfouz's *Arabian Nights and Days* is fiction about fiction; it is a novel built on the original fictitious *The Nights*, a metafiction. Yet Mahfouz's creation is more attached to reality and the contemporary situation while it is still a fiction. *Arabian Nights and Days* is carefully constructed as a contemporary version of *The Nights* using either some of the same generic conventions or parodying other conventions to represent Mahfouz's worldview of the national social and political situation in Egypt.

In his rewriting of the original *Nights*, Mahfouz has a greater advantage than any other Western rewriting or adaptation of this classic. This is because "the true meaning and impact of a fairy tale can be appreciated, its enchantment can be experienced, only from the story in its original form,"[318] and Mahfouz is closer to the original forms of tales in *The Nights* than any Western writer or translator. However, it is well known that, though written in Arabic, different stories and tales in the original *The Nights* have come down from different civilizations: Mesopotamian, Indian, Persian, Arab etc. "If the Arabic 'texts' were the product of cross-cultural exchange, the pervasive global influence of the *Nights* underscores even more the multi-cultural dimensions of their stories."[319] In addition, "Arab writers are now turning to re-writing the *Nights* stories as part of their engagement with cultural and identity politics as well as way of producing 'authentic' Arabic novel."[320] These perplexing ideas point to the fact that Mahfouz's *Arabian Nights and Days* is problematic. It is apparent from the title, subject matter, and characters, that Mahfouz's novel is a contemporary rewriting of the original *Nights*. Yet, it has been presumed that the contemporary Arabic novel is an imported literary genre from the West. Therefore, "Locating the 'authenticity' of modern Arabic story-telling in the *Nights* is interestingly

---

Arabian Nights, nor can we comfortably place the text in a definite historical epoch." (Ghazoul *Nocturnal Poetics* 9)
[317] Thomas D'evelyn 2
[318] Wen-Chin Ouyang 126
[319] Ouyang 127
[320] Ouyang 128

problematic"[321] because it contradicts popular presumption.[322] The contemporary Arabic novel (represented here by Mahfouz's work) followed Western ways of writing fiction for a while. Then, when the West returned, roughly after World War II, to narrative techniques very similar to those in traditional works such as in *The Nights* for example, Arab writers did the same.[323] However, being native speakers of Arabic and being part of the culture that produced what is called medieval texts, Arab writers have a greater advantage than Western writers when adopting literary works originally compiled and written in Arabic such as *The Nights*. This is probably why Mahfouz has his share of precedence of innovation in fiction. It has been explained above that seminal metafictional impulses appear in Mahfouz's fiction beginning with *The Trilogy*.

The second point of difference between the two night-works is point of view. It is the omniscient extradiegetic narrator, not Shahrazad, who narrates all the stories in *Arabian Nights and Days*. By choosing an omniscient narrator, Mahfouz expands the scope of his characters' suffering to include men and women. The personal plight of Shahrazad of the original, *The Nights* (even though it can be applied to the plights of all women) is still limited in comparison to the plight in Mahfouz's novel. The plight has been expanded by Mahfouz to include all the human race, women and men. Mahfouz's tale does not fulfill the promise of its antecedent text—that of saving women from death. Instead, *Arabian Nights and Days* views the whole relationship of governments and the governed through the history of modern Egypt as coincident with death. Due to corruption and the absence of justice, modern man has lost hope. The omniscient extradiegetic narrator of *Arabian Nights and Days* allows Mahfouz to represent different worlds imposing different identities and different roles.

The third point of difference is that Mahfouz's omniscient extradiegetic narrator puts forward what seems to be a continuation of the original, *The Nights*. Mahfouz's novel starts with the wazir being sent for by Shahrayar, and apprehensively the omniscient narrator says:

"Three years he had spent between fear and hope, between death and expectations; three years spent in the telling of stories; and, thanks to those stories, Shahrazad's life span had been extended. Yet, like everything, the stories had come to an end, had ended yesterday."[324]

This quotation is used a second time to explicitly assert that Mahfouz's novel is structured around the original frame story of Shahrazad and Shahrayar, but it

---

[321] Ouyang 125

[322] Naguib Mahfouz says, "Some trace the origins of the Arabic novel back to the Thousand and One Nights, others to Hadith Isa ibn Hisham. Still others believe the novel is a foreign import from nineteenth-century Europe. My first concept of the novel was formed by the Qur'an. It attracted me as a fine form of the art of storytelling. Until today, the stories of the Qur'an have an unparalleled effect on the reader's feelings" (Salmawy Naguib Mahfouz at Sidi Gaber 66).

[323] See above p. 158.

[324] Mahfouz *Arabian Nights and Days* 1

is, in fact, different from it as it picks up from where *The Nights* had stopped at the end of the thousand and one nights of story-telling. The beginning of *Arabian Nights and Days* on the day those thousand and one nights of story-telling finishes is intentionally done in order to explore sufferings of all humans and not only women.

The fourth point of difference is that Mahfouz's work is not divided into nights. The division into nights is a highly important metafictional narrative component of interruption and suspense. The division into nights is an admired narrative device that has guaranteed the longevity of popularity of the original classic throughout the ages. However, several aspects contribute to the elimination of what could be called a default of the missing of the division into nights in Mahfouz's novel. First, *The Nights* serves as the matrix for *Arabian Nights and Days*, as stated above, which could bring down the division into night to Mahfouz's novel even though it does not exist overtly.

Moreover, Mahfouz's choice of title, ليالي ألف ليلة *Layali Alf Laylah*, is self-reflexive of the division into nights in the original title of *The Nights* as it carries the gloomy atmosphere of darkness, uncertainty, and fear. If translated literally, Mahfouz's title would be, *Nights as the Thousand Nights*, or more literally *Nights of the Thousand Nights*.[325] But Denys Jonson-Davies, the translator of Mahfouz's *Nights* alters the title, for reasons not apparent to me, to become *Arabian Nights and Days* even though there is no mention of the words 'Arabian' and 'days' in the original title. The translation loses the connotations associated with the word 'night' in comparison with the word 'day.' Again, if translated correctly, Mahfouz's title would have held a strong implication to the division into nights in the original classic.

Furthermore, in not dividing his novel into nights, Mahfouz's purpose, it seems, is to draw attention to his own vision of the realities of his time. Maybe "Mahfouz appears to have been motivated by a desire to protest the religious traditionalism sweeping across the Arabic-speaking and Muslim world from his native Egypt to Khomeini's Iran."[326] Or, more probably, Mahfouz was protesting the unhealthy political and social atmospheres of Egypt during the second half of the twentieth century. What is relevant here is that Mahfouz's creation presents a narrative world of time as the time of the thousand and one nights where injustice, cruelty, and absolute dominance prevail.

In addition, what is special about Mahfouz in the debate of metafiction and its affinities with *The Nights* is that he is a native speaker of Arabic, a philosophy major graduate, a long practitioner of fiction making, and a Noble Prize winner for his literary achievements. He has, therefore, like John Barth, enough potential, experience, and ability to be "less interested in *The Nights'* formal structure and more preoccupied with developing various thematic concerns that

---

[325] The title given to the work in El-Enany's book *Naguib Mahfouz: The Pursuit of Meaning* published in 1993 before the appearance of the translation of Mahfouz's *Nights* into English

[326] Parreiras-Horta 273

are left implicit in the earlier medieval texts."[327] The condensed *Arabian Nights and Days* represents, therefore, an interesting example when tracing the linguistic and philosophical practices to metafiction that grapples with thematic practices as well. The novel is packed with short precise sentences that have philosophical implications. In the third short chapter of the novel, entitled "The Sheikh," Doctor Abdul Qadir al-Maheeni exchanges conversation with Sheikh Abdullah al-Balkhi when news spread that Shahrayar has decided to marry Shahrazad.

"You have no doubt heard the news?" said Abdul Qadir.
"I know what it is my business to know," he said with a smile.
"Voices are lifted in prayer for Shahrazad, showing that it is you who primarily deserves the credit," said the doctor.
"Credit is for the Beloved alone," he said in reproof.
"I too am a believer, yet I follow promises and deductions. Had she not been a pupil of yours as a young girl, Shahrazad would not, despite what you may say, have found stories to divert the sultan from shedding blood."
"My friend, the only trouble with you is that you overdo submission to the intellect."
"It is the ornament of man."
"It is through intellect that we come to know the limits of the intellect."
"There are believers," said Abdul Qadir, "who are of the opinion that it has no limits."
"I have failed to draw many to the Way—you at the head of them."
"People are poor creatures, master, and are in need of someone to enlighten them about their lives."
"May a righteous soul save a nation," said the sheikh with confidence.[328]

In the next chapter, "The Café of the Emirs," several characters gather, and unidentified, they utter compact sentences full of enthusiasm.

"Let us recite the Fatiha over the souls of the victims," several voices rang out.
"Of virgins and God-fearing men."
"Farewell to tears."
"Praise and thanks be to God, Lord of the Worlds."
"And a long life to Shahrazad, the pearl of women."
"Thanks to those beautiful stories."
"It is nothing but God's mercy that has descended."[329]

In these two linguistically and philosophically packed quotations, a lot has been said with few words. The story of Shahrazad and Shahrayar is mentioned,

---

[327] David Pinault "Naguib Mahfouz" 312
[328] Mahfouz *Arabian Nights and Days* 6
[329] Mahfouz *Arabian Nights and Days* 9

the concept of theism and faith (in general) are discussed, the limits of human knowledge and intellect is discussed, the human need for guidance is there, and the recognition of the value of story-telling is also there. In spite of the differences between *The Nights* and Mahfouz's *Arabian Nights and Days*, the compacted structure of Mahfouz's novel allows the presence of all these themes.

Instead of the division into nights, Mahfouz's novel has a unique metafictional structure of self-reflexivity in that Mahfouz is directing his reader to the fictional work, *The Nights*. In place of a recognizable plot, the novel has the frame story of Shahrazad and Shahrayar of *The Nights* as matrix and as starting point. Mahfouz builds upon there a fragmented text of 17 narrative blocks, each crowned with a title. The first four, which are only about few hundred words each, introduce the most important elements of the whole text: the wazir Dandan, Shahrayar, Shahrazad, Sheikh Abdullah al-Balkhi, and the café of the Emirs. These elements will be analyzed respectively.

It is implied from the beginning of the novel that the thousand and one nights of story-telling are over with Shahrayar deciding to spare Shahrazad's life and marry her officially. Ironically, the deliverer of the good news, which makes the narrative of the first chapter, is the same wazir who used to implement Shahrayar's orders of the executions of young brides before Shahrayar met Shahrazad. The wazir, father of Shahrazad, gets more attention by Mahfouz than in the original *Nights*. The grand wazir, father of Shahrazad, has never been named in *The Nights*, but in Mahfouz's novel his name is Dandan.[330] Dandan is the wazir of King Umar, the great wise heroic figure in "Sirat Umar ibn al-Nu'man" (which appears in nights 44 through 145 in the Cairo-Bulaq edition of *The Nights*). Ferial Ghazoul in her book, *The Arabian Nights: A Structural Analysis* says that in this *Sira* there is struggle between believers and non-believers as the whole narrative is "a story of the eventual triumph of Islam against its enemies. This is what happens in the end."[331] Mahfouz may have intentionally used the name to draw attention to "Sirat Umar ibn al-Nu'man" which is built upon the political struggle between East and West in terms of religious beliefs. This religious-base struggle is the basic cause of turbulence in the contemporary Egypt of Mahfouz. In giving the wazir of Shahrayar a name, Mahfouz, in *Arabian Nights and Days*, metafictionally produces a reflexive art that imitates other arts.

The relationship between Shahrayar and the wazir Dandan becomes, therefore, more significant to establish "a classic Mahfouzian theme: the question of how to achieve right governance and the proper use of authority by those who dominate society."[332] Usually, there is positive or negative impact of persons around authority; if a wazir is good and just, the head of authority will

---

[330] The grand wazir is also given a name, Nur-al Din, in Bakathir's play, Sir Shahrazad. In Al-Hakim's play, Shahrazad, the wazir is also given a name, Qamar. This could be an indication of the continued influence of contemporary Eastern texts related to The Nights upon each other.

[331] Ghazoul *A Structural Analysis* 77

[332] Pinault "Naguib Mahfouz" 312

be affected by him. The wazir's name and place in the narrative as the one who breaks the good news to Shahrazad and to the world are indication of the possible impact he plays.

Shahrayar, on the other hand, is restless. Everybody in the city is overjoyed by his decision except him. Shahrayar is no longer occupied with Shahrazad and her stories. After that matter is settled, he is concerned about his sultanate and imposing justice in it as he says to his wazir, "Existence itself is the most inscrutable thing in existence" (*Arabian Nights and Days* 2). Preoccupied with the meaning of existence, Mahfouz's Shahrayar is out of his palace and out of the realm of the fiction of Shahrazad's stories and into the realm of reality of his time and place. But that reality is also fictitious; this forms layers of fiction upon fiction. In spite of its fictionality, Mahfouz's realm is a step closer to reality and to metafiction as it depicts the contemporary social and political situation of Egypt. *Arabian Nights and Days* is "a political allegory very few can doubt."[333] Mahfouz gets Shahrayar out of his palace and places him among his people where he actually belongs, worrying about justice and social order. Unlike in *The Nights*, especially after Shahrazad begins her long thousand and one nights of story-telling and Shahrayar only listens to her, Mahfouz enables Shahrayar to play a bigger role. Mahfouz's Shahrayar is an active central character who has changed, probably because of those endless nights of story-telling. However, neither Shahrazad nor Dandan, his wazir and one of the closest to him, are sure of that change that gets a chance to be tested after some social turbulence. According to the extradiegetic narrator, Dandan was always asking himself whether the sultan had truly changed or whether it was a passing phase. But be patient. In the past he had been decisive, clear, cruel, and insensitive. Now a perplexed look was quick to flash in his eyes.

"The nation is happy and profuse in its thanks," said Dandan.
"Ali al-Salouli was murdered," muttered the sultan sharply, "and was quickly followed by Khalil al-Hamadani."
"Good and evil are like day and night," said Dandan with compassion.
"And the genies?"
"When faced with the leather mat of execution a criminal makes up what story he can."
"But I remember the stories of Shahrazad," he said quietly.
Dandan's heart beat fast and he said, "A murderer must meet his punishment."
"The truth is that I was on the point of contenting myself with imprisoning Gamasa al-Balti." Then wrathfully, "But I executed him as a penalty for his insolent way of addressing me."
Dandan told himself that his master had changed only superficially.[334]

---

[333] Ghazoul *Nocturnal Poetics* 138
[334] Mahfouz *Arabian Nights and Days* 55

Feeling that his power is restricted because of his limited ability to restore peace and order, Shahrayar wanders in his city disguised as a merchant only to be faced with treachery, corruption, injustice, and unbelievable incidents to the point of finding a false Sultan. These events and incidents refer to similar somehow real incidents in modern Egypt. However, the complexity of Mahfouz's novel in mixing the ordinary with the supernatural makes decoding difficult. In Mahfouz's novel, the mode of encoding depends on orienting the fantastic incidents—drawn from the repertoire of *The Arabian Nights*—to point to actual events and scandals, commonly circulating among the people but panned from press mention. It is Mahfouz's talent for charging the fabulous and fantastic with the familiar and the actual that turns the marvelous dimension on its head.[335]

In the novel's last narrative, "The Grievers," the character of Shahrayar gets its last development. This narrative which "concludes the frame story"[336] represents Shahrayar's search for eternal happiness, and when he finds it he makes the mistake of losing it. In this closing chapter, Mahfouz dramatizes the character Shahrayar using the metafictional technique of self-reflexivity of another narrative, Adam's fall from heaven.

Shahrazad's character, on the other hand, is less present in Mahfouz's *Nights* than in the original, *The Nights*. Shahrazad had learned her stories from Abdullah al-Balkhi, a Sufi sheikh. "Throughout this work the sheikh's serenity acts as a counterpoint to Shahriyar's restlessness."[337] Shahrazad no longer needs to tell stories as Shahrayar has decided to marry her. Nevertheless, she is unhappy and patiently staying with him following the teachings of the great Sheikh from whom she had got her thousand and one nights' stories. Nevertheless, the value of her role as story-teller is magnified at the near end of the novel. One night after hearing Sinbad's stories and feeling bored, Shahrayar and Shahrazad exchange the long but important discussion:

"A wise man does not become bored, Your Majesty," she said with concern.
"I?" he asked with annoyance. "Wisdom is a difficult requirement—it is not inherited as a throne is."
"The city today enjoys your upright wisdom."
"And the past, Shahrazad?"
"True repentance wipes away the past."
"Even if the ruler concerned himself with killing innocent young girls and the cream of the men of judgment?"
"True repentance..." she said in a trembling voice.
"Don't try to deceive me, Shahrazad," he interrupted her.
"But, Majesty, I am telling the truth."
"The truth," he said with resolute roughness, "is that your body approaches while your heart turns away."

---

[335] Ghazoul *Nocturnal Poetics* 139
[336] Ghazoul *Nocturnal Poetics* 141
[337] Pinault "Naguib Mahfouz" 313

She was alarmed—it was as if she had been stripped naked in the darkness.

"Your Majesty!" she called out in protest.

"I am not wise but also I am not stupid. How often I have been aware of your contempt and aversion!"

"God knows…" she said, her voice torn with emotion, but he interrupted her. "Don't lie, and don't be afraid. You have lived with a man who was steeped in blood of martyrs."

"We all extol your merits."

Without heeding her words, he said, "Do you know why I kept you close by me? Because I found in your aversion a continued torment that I deserved. What saddens me is that I believe that I deserve punishment."

She could not stop herself from crying and he said gently, "Weep, Shahrazad, for weeping is better than lying."[338]

The above introduction to the last narrative, "The Grievers,"[339] is a unit of discourse that explicitly deals with the relationship of Shahrazad and Shahrayar. Shahrazad is unhappy even though she tries to hide her feelings. Shahrazad's feeling of distress in Mahfouz's work is picked up by Barth in his work *Ten Nights*, which is proof of the effect of *Arabian Nights and Days* on the development of metafiction.[340]

Near the end of *Arabian Nights and Days*, Mahfouz's Shahrayar hands Shahrazad the responsibility of disciplining her son, the new sultan, to be a good and just ruler. Upon departing, Shahrayar says:

"The palace is yours," he said in protest, "and that of your son who will be ruling the city tomorrow. It is I who must go, bearing my bloody past."

"Majesty!"

"For the space of ten years I have lived torn between temptation and duty: I remember and I pretend to have forgotten; I show myself as refined and I lead a dissolute life; I proceed and I forget; I advance and I retreat; and in all circumstances I am tormented. The time has come for me to listen to the call of salvation, the call of wisdom."

"You are spurning me as my heart opens to you," she said in a tone of avowal.

"I no longer look to the hearts of humankind," he said sternly.

"It is an opposing destiny that is mocking us."

"We must be satisfied with what has been fated for us."

"My natural place is as your shadow," she said bitterly.

"The sultan," he said with a calm unaffected by emotions, "must depart once he has lost competence; as for ordinary man, he must find his salvation."

"You are exposing the city to horrors."

---

[338] Mahfouz *Arabian Nights and Days* 216–17

[339] El-Enany translates it more accurately into 'The Weepers' in his 1993 book *Naguib Mahfouz: The Pursuit of Meaning*

[340] See above, p. 148–50.

"Rather am I opening to it the door of purity, while I wander about aimlessly seeking my salvation."

She stretched out her hand toward his in the darkness, but he withdrew his own with the words. "Get up and proceed to your task. You have disciplined the father and you must prepare the son for a better outcome."[341]

These long quotations must be included as they beautifully summarize the relationship of Mahfouz's main characters, Shahrayar and Shahrazad, with each other and with the dominating theme of Mahfouz's novel, which is authority and how man observes and deals with it in order to implement justice. Ironically, to implement justice Mahfouz's novel proposes handing down the responsibility of raising and educating the new sultan to a woman, which reveals Mahfouz's stand on women. They are, in his point of view, capable of paving the ground for justice through raising better citizens. After that conversation, Mahfouz's Shahrayar "abandoned throne and glory, woman and child. He deposed himself, defeated before his heart's revolt at a time when his people had forgotten his past misdeeds."[342] Shahrazad's role and that of all women in that respect, therefore, have been greatly emphasized by Mahfouz's *Nights* as positive and practical in order to reach social balance.

The sheikh, Abdullah al-Balkhi, is another central character in *Arabian Nights and Days*. His importance to the development of the novel is apparent as Mahfouz assigns him the third brief chapter. He is the wise sheikh who taught Shahrazad all the stories she narrated in the original, *The Nights*, and he is the Sheikh of the Way whose influence spread on not only Shahrazad and Shahrayar but also on all good characters in *Arabian Nights and Days*. He "stands for spiritual power and love."[343] His friend Abdul Qadir al-Maheeni stands for the power of science and human knowledge. Al-Maheeni visits the sheikh when the news of Shahrayar marrying Shahrazad spread. The two exchange a conversation full of philosophical remarks on human guidance. The two characters, the sheikh and al-Maheeni, stand for opposing factors that pull society members towards religious beliefs or secular beliefs. Their presence is necessary to highlight pressures Mahfouz's Shahrayar is suffering from. The representative of religion and mysticism, the sheikh, is also a refuge for the occupants of the city whenever they are faced with an inexplicable circumstance. The three central characters, Shahrayar, Shahrazad, and the sheikh, according to Ghazoul, stand for three allegorized notions: political power, creative power, and mystic power. In order for political power to be successful and balanced, it not only needs strength but also creativity/knowledge and mysticism.

Mahfouz's world of *Arabian Nights and Days* has a fourth introductory chapter, "The Café of the Emirs," which provides the setting. "It is a microcosm of the city/Egypt/the world; it is a café where all classes—upper and lower—meet, although they are distinguished by the seats they sit on, which vary from

---

[341] Mahfouz *Arabian Nights and Days* 217–218
[342] Mahfouz *Arabian Nights and Days* 222
[343] Ghazoul *Nocturnal Poetics* 140

comfortable sofas to pads on the floor."[344] Almost all characters of Mahfouz's *Arabian Nights and Days* meet in this café. Mahfouz, however, metafictionally situates this setting within the time of the original *Nights*. Therefore, the effect "is a widening of the scope of the author's vision beyond historical and geographical borders. Myth, in addition, probably works better on the reader's subconscious than a realistic representation of reality."[345]

This chapter together with the other three short introductory chapters display metafictional techniques of reflexivity of other narratives, of real events, and of fictional settings. In addition to metafictional techniques, Mahfouz uses some techniques of modernism such as symbolism, recurrent motifs, stream of consciousness, and even a kind of magical realism.[346] This mixture of style is distinctive of Mahfouz.

After the four introductory chapters, Mahfouz's *Arabian Nights and Days* is structured around another dozen chapters, each with a major tale; the novel then ends up with a concluding chapter. All twelve tales, which are "originally independent of each other are so manipulated that they join in a narrative continuum."[347] These twelve tales "evoke deteriorating values, ruling repression, corruption, hypocrisy, and opportunism."[348] Ghazoul adds in the same source that "the mode of encoding depends on orienting the fantastic incidents—drawn from the repertoire of *The Arabian Nights*—to point to actual events and scandals, commonly circulating among the people but banned from press mention." Mahfouz makes use of these twelve tales to tie *Arabian Nights and Days* to the realities of contemporary Egypt, and Barth in his *Ten Nights* picks up this relation to realities in tying his work to the realities of the 9/11 events.

"San'aan Al-Gamali," the first of the twelve is the tale of a good merchant who commits rape and murder under the influence of a genie. Al-Gamali is confused to the extent that the narrator asks, "Was it the genie? Was it the dope he had swallowed? Or was it San'aan al-Gamali?"[349] What happens to San'aan is a mixture between dream and reality or rather a magical reality; it is a kind of misfortune beyond his will, and it leads to his execution and ruining of his family. This swinging between dreams, reality, and metaphysical and human entities takes this tale into the realm of metafiction.

"Gamsa Al-Balti" is the tale of the chief of police who, while fishing, is also influenced by another genie whom he frees from captivity in a steel ball. Instead of rewarding Gamsa for freeing him from his captivity (which is what usually happens in fairy tales), the genie decides to punish Gamsa for disturbing his peaceful sleep and bringing him to this unstable world! However, the genie postpones the punishment of Gamsa. When Gamsa returns to shore, he finds that the servant waiting for him did not see the smoke gathering to be the genie even

---

[344] Ghazoul *Nocturnal Poetics* 140
[345] El-Enany *The Pursuit of Meaning* 160
[346] El-Enany *The Pursuit of Meaning* 160
[347] El-Enany *The Pursuit of Meaning* 160
[348] Ghazoul *Nocturnal Poetics* 139
[349] Mahfouz *Arabian Nights and Days* 19

though he was watching his master all the time. It is Gamsa only that witnesses that genie which is an indication from Mahfouz that genies are within a person and are not external forces. Meeting the genie is an interesting experience that changes his life from a corrupt person into a good man who has to be killed for his bad deeds. Gamsa is killed, but his soul lives in another body, the body of "The Porter." In this tale, Abdullah the porter, who was Gamsa Al-Balti, is questioning the meaning of his existence in a new body. He goes to Sheikh Abdullah Al-Balkhi for an answer. Then, "he told himself that the sheikh was privy to his apprehensions and had brought him back to himself. This he must accept"[350] since Adam, the father of man, has accepted the responsibility of intelligence. Abdullah the porter is also faced with a genie who acknowledges the change in his personality towards fighting evil by killing evil people. His identity changes again after meeting Abdullah of the sea; he becomes Abdullah of the land, the mad man. The continuous encounter with the supernatural in these tales and in another tale, "The Adventures of Ugr the Barber," is a narrative device of metafiction.

As an assertion of the idea that the origin of good and evil is within a person, the character, the madman, continues to operate among tales until the near end of the novel as the voice of reason in a world that does not see it as such. In the tale, "Nur Al-Din and Dunyazad," two evil genies, Zarmabaha and Sakhrabout, also have a role. They work, through playful dreams, to bring the young and handsome ordinary citizen Nur Al-Din with Dunyazad, sister of Shahrazad, in a passionate relationship. When Dunyazad awakens from her near-real dream, she goes to her sister Shahrazad to tell her about it. Shahrazad says,

> *"What man of sense would accept your story?"*
> *"That is what I tell myself. It is a story like one of your amazing tales."*
> *"My tales are derived from another world, Dunyazad."*
> *"I have fallen prisoner to the truth of your mysterious world, but I do not want to be its victim."[351]*

The metafictional device of playfulness of the mixture between dream and reality appears in "Nur Al-Din and Dunyazad" using magic, mystery, and dreams, bringing two people from two different sectors of society together against all odds. In addition, the explicit reference to story-telling is yet another metafictional technique at work in this tale. It is also at work in another tale, as "Anees Al-Galees" opens with Shahrayar conversing with his wazir Dandan about the value of narration. Shahrayar says, "Shahrazad has taught me to believe what man's logic gives the lie to…and to plunge into a sea of contradictions. Whenever night comes it seems to me that I am a poor man."[352] Moreover, in these two tales, as in other tales in *Arabian Nights and Days*, Mahfouz's narrative

---

[350] Mahfouz *Arabian Nights and Days* 58
[351] Mahfouz *Arabian Nights and Days* 82
[352] Mahfouz *Arabian Nights and Days* 131

world intertwines with the narrative world of *The Nights* creating a metafictional text.

"Aladdin with the Moles on His Cheeks" also connotes *The Nights* in the character Aladdin who mirrors Aladdin of *The Nights*, in the inclusion of dreams, and in the occupation with narration. Also, this tale's compacted introductory chapter that has a fragmented nature reflects Mahfouz's talent of constructing narratives:

In the quietness of the night Gamsa al-Balti called out from under the date palm. "O God, free me from yesterday. O God, free me from tomorrow."
Then Singam's voice was heard: "We love what you love, but between us and people is a barrier of destinies."
The laughter of Zarambaha rang out, "Why were honey and wine created?"
Shahrayar was going about his nightly peregrinations with his two men.
"Continuous whisperings pass through me, but my head spins in a state of bewilderment," he said to Dandan.[353]

Mahfouz in this tale also uses the element of dream philosophically to refer to the political realities of suppression in Egypt at the time of the production of *Arabian Nights and Days*:

"Let your beard grow." Aladdin was amazed at this request, and the madman said, "It is only a snare for hunting."
"But I am a barber not a hunter," said Aladdin.
"Man was created to be a hunter," shouted the madman.[354]

After the dream, Aladdin changes as an indication of the power of dreams in fiction.

The tale, "The Sultan," gives the discovery by Shahrayar, of a parallel sultanate on a nearby island with a sultan whose name is also Shahrayar and events and citizens like those in the real Shahrayar's sultanate. The difference is that the replica is a place where justice prevails. This tale is interesting as it is metafiction that "paints a landscape for the reader [or the character Shahrayar in this context] and encourages him to include himself in the painting and stand back to view himself."[355] When the so-called real Shahrayar witnesses, through this narratively painted replica, the other side of things, he takes actions so justice prevails in his own sultanate. "The Sultan," as a whole, is a metafictional mixture between fiction and reality.

"The Cap of Invisibility" is the only tale, from the twelve, that does not carry the name of its main protagonist, Fadil San'aan. Instead, it carries the name of a device, the cap of invisibility, which was fictionally invented to enable characters to have freedom. Under the influence of invisibility, Fadil changes to perform

---

[353] Mahfouz *Arabian Nights and Days* 157
[354] Mahfouz *Arabian Nights and Days* 161
[355] Heckard 211

acts the evil side of him desires like theft, mockery, murder, drinking, adultery, and escape from prison. Fadil becomes a slave to invisibility and to the genie who gave it to him, but his good nature finally wins and he removes the cap and accepts his execution. This tale has an element of metafiction as it is fiction about fiction.

"Ma'rouf the Cobbler," is the tale of a layman who "One night . . . swallowed an excess of narcotics and went off to the Café of the Emirs with the world not big enough to contain his feeling of well-being."[356] Being high, he pretends to have found the ring of Solomon (another fictional device) and performs an act of magic to prove it. It turns out that a genie is the one who gave him the powerful magic of the ring. With the proposed power of the ring, Ma'rouf acquires happiness and wealth, and is able to gain the respect of people through helping the poor. The last chapter of his tale shows Shahrayar appointing Ma'rouf the position of governor for his good nature in using power. "Ma'rouf the Cobbler," therefore is fiction about fiction that proposes the power of fiction in bringing happiness and people's respect.

In the last tale of the twelve, "Sinbad," the power of fiction and reference to story-telling are metafictional techniques Mahfouz uses. Sinbad the sailor returns from his seven voyages to tell Shahrayar of the wisdom he acquired. Sinbad stories are so effective on Shahrayar that they represent the straw that broke Shahrayar's back, so to speak. In Mahfouz's *Arabian Nights and Days*, therefore, it is not only Shahrazad's stories that change Shahrayar. They are also those twelve stories that transform Shahrayar from a tyrannical ruler into a good and kind man. The extradiegetic narrator explains the situation of Shahrayar while he wanders at night:

Voices from the past pressed in on his ears, erasing the melodies of the garden; the cheers of victory, the roars of anger, the groans of virgins, the raging of believers, the singing of hypocrites, and the calling of God's name from atop the minarets. The falseness of spacious glory was made clear to him, like a mask of tattered paper that does not conceal the snakes of cruelty, tyranny, pillage, and blood that lie behind it. He cursed his father and his mother, the givers of pernicious legal judgments and the poets, the cavaliers of deception, the robbers of the treasury, the whores from noble families, and the gold that was plundered and squandered on glasses of wine, elaborate turbans, fancy walls, and furniture, empty hearts and the suicidal soul, and the derisive laughter of the universe.[357]

Upon returning, Shahrayar summons Shahrazad to tell her that Sinbad stories are like hers, and she says, "All originate from a single source, Your Majesty."[358] That source seems pressing on Sinbad as he yearns, near end of his tale, for travel recognizing the value of experience which would be transferred into narration.

---

[356] Mahfouz *Arabian Nights and Days* 194
[357] Mahfouz *Arabian Nights and Days* 216
[358] Mahfouz *Arabian Nights and Days* 216

This is a clever Mahfouzian hint that narratives, reflexive of other narratives, have a goal of living across time. In other words, Mahfouz hints that his own *Nights* is yet a ring in the chain of narrative adjacent to the chain of being: Mahfouz's "characters continue to operate across tales and meet up with other characters, unlike in the original, while completely new characters and events are invented and incorporated in the book to serve the novelist's goals."[359]

Character from the modern *Nights*, that are not in the original, exchange conversation with Sinbad:

"It is as though I have received a call from beyond the seas."
"Travel," said Abdul Qadir al-Maheeni simply. "For in journeys there are numberless benefits."
"I saw in a dream the roc fluttering its wings," said Sinbad.
"Perhaps it is invitation to the skies," said the sheikh.
"I am a man of seas and islands," said Sinbad submissively.[360]

Mahfouz's twelve tales, except one, carry the names of their protagonists in the same fashion of Mahfouz's earlier work, *Mirrors*. However, *Mirrors* seems systematically more close to metafiction as it is fragmentally structured around tales that stand independently and it is open-ended. Tales of *Arabian Nights and Days*, on the other hand, seem more attached and more modern. Their characters and events intertwine across tales to produce the outcome of the whole narrative. But, since *Arabian Nights and Days* is a metafictional novel built upon *The Nights*, this unified appearance is misleading as "the narrative strategies of metafictional texts operate to assert dissident cultural values."[361] Therefore, in spite of modern appearance, its metafictionality is dominating for the many reasons explained above.

Towards the end of the novel, Mahfouz closes *Arabian Nights and Days* with the tale, "The Grievers." Although the original, *The Nights*, has what Ghazoul calls "virtual ending" which has motivated writers to write the thousand and second night of story-telling, Mahfouz does not fall into that motivation. His last tale, "The Grievers," "concludes the frame story…and provides the key to comprehending the allegory in the book."[362] All in all, Mahfouz's treatment of 'the art of nights' differs from the treatment of Barth in *Ten Nights and a Night: Eleven Stories*. Barth's work is immersed in the metafictionality of the process of writing fiction to the extent of producing a loose work that fails to keep the interest of the reader. Although still metafictional, Mahfouz's novel is carefully constructed to start at the controversial open-ended conclusion of *The Nights*, which holds the interest of its reader to see what happens to Shahrayar.

To conclude this chapter, it suffices to say that Mahfouz's contribution to the development of fiction nationally and internationally is recognizable through his

---

[359] El-Enany *His Life and Times* 131
[360] Mahfouz *Arabian Nights and Days* 219
[361] Stirling "Neurotic Narrative" 2
[362] Ghazoul *Nocturnal Poetics* 141

innovative fiction that won him the highest literary prize, fame, and acclaim. From an early stage in his writing career, Mahfouz was occupied not solely with events and characters that have captured the interest of writers of fiction during the modern period but with the passage of time and how it affects individuals and their actions as the postmodern writers try to highlight. One of the first critics to recognize Mahfouz's preoccupation with time is Trevor LeGassick in his 1963 article, "Najib Mahfouz' Trilogy." He says: "Neither Najib Mahfouz' trilogy nor several of his other works have a 'hero' or obviously central figure as do the majority of novels… Mahfouz commented in a recent interview that time itself was the hero of his novels."[363] The centrality of the concept of time in Mahfouz's work is also thoroughly examined by Rasheed El-Enany who acknowledges that Mahfouz's perception then concentration on the passage of time had led him to see the constraints of realism and modernism on writing fiction. It has opened doors for him to innovation and precedence towards the development of metafiction.

Metafiction, therefore, has developed with time from an application of a narrow path of experimentation during the 1960s and the 1970s, into a wide array of techniques where the construction of narratives, like those of Mahfouz, is governed by order and not chaos. Mahfouz's fiction, throughout his development as writer of fiction, has enriched the interaction between East and West. Since he won the Nobel Prize in literature in 1988, more and more of Mahfouz's fiction has been translated into foreign languages. Mahfouz now is a prominent literary figure whose fiction is part of the international literary theory. It is important to note that the applications of metafictional techniques have changed as "Theories and interpretive practices change with time, reflecting changing worldviews and uses of literature."[364] This calls for a change in literary theory to include not only literature produced in the West but also literature produced in other parts of the world.

---

[363] Trevor LeGassick 66
[364] John Lye 90

Chapter IV
Barth's Ten Nights and a Night:
Eleven Stories and Metafiction

The interest of this book so far is the development and theorization of metafiction and its presence in *The Book of the Thousand and One Nights*. The two, metafiction and *The Nights*, have been explored by John Barth, the American novelist, short story writer, and critic, for most of his writing career. In order to add to the subject of metafiction, this chapter deals with Barth's preoccupation with the two subjects until he wrote his work, *Ten Nights and a Night: Eleven Stories* published in 2004, where the connection between metafiction and the original *Nights* is further illuminated.

John Simmons Barth (1930-) is not only a writer of fiction and a critic but he has also been a teacher of English then a professor of creative writing for more than five decades until his retirement in 2003. Barth has been recognized as one of the major writers occupied with experimentation in literature which was later theorized as metafiction. His preoccupation with experimentation started to appear in his fiction and nonfiction roughly from the beginning of the 1960s. Before then, his first two novels, *The Floating Opera* (1956), and *The End of the Road* (1958), are considered "relatively realistic."[365] Barth's next novel, *The Sot-Weed Factor* (1960) reveals a change in narrative style. This novel marks the beginning of Barth's passion for the fictional technique of storytelling to explain past and present facts of life. This novel is "not so much a book about history or historical characters as about the nature of storytelling."[366] The composition of *The Sot-Weed Factor*, according to Jac Tharpe, "provided him [Barth] with a great experience in maturation of both form and content... He had been automatically concerned with the matter of epistemology..."[367] With this novel, Barth began to explore the relationship of knowledge, any type of knowledge, to personal experiences. The idea that "nothing has intrinsic value appears to remain valid throughout Barth's work to date."[368] It is also well known that "in the 1960s John Barth made recourse to the *Nights* in his fiction and essays to develop a style and theory of writing that would help define postmodern

---

[365] Christensen 58

[366] Christensen 59

[367] Jac Tharpe 4

[368] Tharpe 8

literature."[369] Barth's use of *The Nights* to pass through his philosophical stance directs attention to treasures in this classic as a source of tools suitable for expressing personal values. Interestingly, though, the idea that exploring the philosophical value of personal experiences rather than relying on grand narratives in search of truth was dominating in works with innovative works with metafictional characteristics in the 1960s. It was observed that knowledge is partial and situated, and there is not one truth as everything is affected by culture, class, and gender. These ideas are prominent in works such as Thomas Pynchon's *V.* (1963), *The Crying of Lot 49* (1966), William H. Gass's *In the Heart of the Heart of the Country* (1968), and John Updike's *Rabbit, Run* (1960), just to name a few.

The philosophical value of personal experience is further explored in Barth's next novel, *Giles Goat-Boy* (1966), where a young man's biography reveals his satirical attempts to become a hero. In this novel, Barth continually mocks traditional myths and religious concepts giving more value to personal experience. One year before the publication of *Giles Goat-Boy* Barth asserted his insistence on literary experimentation with the appearance of one of his famous articles, "Muse, Spare Me" (1965), which reveals one of his major sources of inspiration, *The Nights* and Shahrazad in particular. In his article, he says, "The whole frame of those thousand nights and a night speaks to my heart directly and intimately—and in many ways at once, personal and technical."[370] Praising Shahrazad, he says:

My love affair with Scheherazade is an old and continuing one. As an illiterate undergraduate, I worked off part of my tuition filing books in the Classic Library at Johns Hopkins, which included the stacks of the Oriental Seminary… Most of those spellbinding liars I have forgotten, but never Scheherazade.[371]

"Muse, Spare Me" reveals Barth's fondness of Shahrazad and *The Nights*, and it also shows that Barth is an important literary figure with talent and vast knowledge of past literature. He, therefore, could or would play a major role in shaping contemporary theory through his fiction and nonfiction works. Luis Paulo Parreiras-Horta, in his dissertation *Mirrors of Ink and Wonderful Lamps: The Arabian Nights in Victorian and Postmodern Literature* says that Barth in "Muse, Spare Me" used the *Nights* to define an alternative trajectory that would take American fiction in a direction quite different from that of the Black Humorists praised by Knickerbocker. Rather than address "the Madness of Contemporary Society," the writer ought to eschew "contemporaneous, 'original' material" and adopt Shahrazad's practice of inheriting her tales "from the literal and legendary foretime." Rather than be impressed "by the apocalyptic character of the present age" defined in terms of "Modern Warfare" and "Life With the Bomb," this fiction should learn from Shahrazad's predicament—

---

[369] Parreiras-Horta 139
[370] Barth *Friday Book* 56
[371] Barth *Friday Book* 57

"publish or perish"—that "all apocalypses are ultimately personal," for "even mankind's demise will have to consist of each of our dyings."[372]

Parreiras-Horta may have found in Barth's article one of the origins of Barth's realization of the value of personal experience in fiction. There are other works of fiction with frame narratives, but Barth prefers *The Nights* because it is "darker, more magical and dreamish."[373] Unlike other works of fiction, the dreamy magical qualities are inherent in *The Nights* itself, according to Barth, and are not results of external temporal or spatial influences as the case was for the Existentialists and Black Humorists in the 1950s and 60s who immersed themselves and their fiction in the problems that prevailed during those two decades. Barth has tried some of this philosophical and humoristic approach in his novel *Giles Goat-Boy*, but he never went as far as refusing to belong to any school of thought or to believe in anything. The influence of the French Jean-Paul Sartre, Albert Camus, Simone de Beauvoir, and the German American philosopher Walter Kaufman was strong, but Barth did not follow their radical thinking and remained neutral in his literary productions. Barth's fiction reveals that personal experiences are celebrated, but refusal of social, mythical, and metaphysical values is unacceptable.

In 1967, Barth published another famous article, "The Literature of Exhaustion," where he discusses the state of narration at that time of change. In the article Barth discusses, among other ideas, Jorge Luis Borges' work because Borges' admiration of *The Nights* was a source of inspiration and innovation for Barth and Borges as well. *The Nights* has been, therefore, a field of mutual interest for both authors known for their precedence in metafictional experimentations. Through the discussion of Borges, "The Literature of Exhaustion" carries Barth's assertion that literature in the modern era is exhausted and it needs to go back to Greek and Oriental classics of the past such as *The Nights* to be fit for the metafiction of the postmodern era.

The following year, 1968, Barth's highly experimental short-story collection, *Lost in the Funhouse* appeared and took the literary milieu by surprise. It shows another facet of metafiction as it "deals explicitly with fictional techniques and experiments in narration."[374] For example, "Lost in the Funhouse," the story, mixes fiction with the process of writing fiction. In *Lost in the Funhouse* Barth self reflexively plays with the writing process and the tools of story-telling in order to mock both writing and fiction as techniques and as art. Coming after "The Literature of Exhaustion," *Lost in the Funhouse* shows another facet of Barth, which is the exploration of one more possible way of expression in fiction which is going back to past literary classics. For instance, in "Menelaiad," a story in this work, Barth parodies the Greek epic form. However, Hierl says, "*Lost in the Funhouse* includes the concern about the exhaustion of content, that is, the feeling that everything has already been said and done and that original thought

---

[372] Parreiras-Horta 141
[373] Barth *Friday Book* 58
[374] Tharpe 10

and art has become impossible."[375] This view may not be completely accurate as Barth is using Oriental and Greek narratives to reject modern logic that dismisses myths and metaphysics. From another perspective, Barth, in his fiction in general and in *Lost in the Funhouse* in particular, is more concerned about form without dismissing content. In his notes to *Lost in the Funhouse*, Barth says:

"This book differs in two ways from most volumes of short fiction. First, it's neither a collection nor a selection, but a series, though several of its items have appeared separately in periodicals, the series will be seen to have been meant to be received 'all at once' and as here arranged. Most of its members, consequently, are 'new'—written for this book, in which they appear for the first time. Second, while some of these pieces were composed expressly for print, others are not…"[376]

In spite of the success of *Lost in the Funhouse*, its highly experimental narrative techniques that rely more on form did not appear in Barth's fiction later on even though he has "The Literature of Exhaustion" to back it up. It seems that the maturing author, Barth, is achieving a better balance between form and content to express the value of personal experience. This is why he probably includes Greek mythology and *The Nights* for his exploration of art and life in his next novel, *Chimera* published in 1972.

Chimera, in this sense, represents an important turning point in Barth's fiction. After the end of the 1960s, the author and his reader were more at ease in accepting postmodern changes with metafictional techniques. There was, therefore, no longer a fear of the exhaustion of the novel form when inspiration is available in great works of the past. In addition, "Whereas *Lost in the Funhouse* was still characterized by a more pessimistic view of the future of fiction, *Chimera* marks Barth's movement toward a more optimistic theory of the novel."[377] This is so because Barth has reached a relaxing balance between form and content through inspirations he could get from Oriental and ancient Greek works. Major writers and nonprofessionals alike have appreciated these ancient works for centuries. These ancient works have carried the experiences of mankind; they helped in shaping the consciousness of great literary figures. John Milton's *Paradise Lost* starts by asking a muse to give inspiration. In ancient Greek and Roman mythology, there were nine sister muses that inspire poets, and Barth got that, with a muse frequently present in his work. In many of his works, Barth's muse is the Oriental Shahrazad of *The Nights*. Barth's references to these great Greek and Oriental classics open up his creations to include not only temporal and spatial upheavals but also infinite human experiences.

In *Chimera*, Barth writes three loosely related novellas that have echoes of other literary classics. *Dunyazadiad*, echoes *The Nights* in frame story and in characters, Shahrazad and Dunyazad, and in the concept of a genie coming from our modern world and writing *Chimera*. The Genie-writer helps Shahrazad by telling her stories she could narrate at night. *Perseid*, the second novella, is

---

[375] Hierl 48

[376] Barth *Lost in the Funhouse* ix

[377] Hierl 49

referential of Greek mythology of the story of Perseus and Medusa when fate, courage, and heroism dominate at last. *Bellerphoniad*, the third novella in *Chimera*, has the name Bellerophon who was able, in mythology, to slay the nasty monster, Chimera. But Barth changes the name to Bellerphoniad in an interesting move. That change of name plus the structure of *Chimera* of these three novellas with one having an Oriental name and the other two having Greek names indicate that Barth views the ancient human artistic creations as one and universal regardless of where they have originated from, East or West. The addition of the suffix, 'iad' to the names Dunyazad and Bellerophon is Barth's way of directing the reader's attention to more possible universal meanings.

It is apparent, fairly clearly, that with *Chimera*, Barth has found his way through technique aided by content, mostly through Shahrazad and *The Nights*, and through Greek and Roman mythology to his reader's attention. In *Chimera*, from one perspective, "Technique is all that one can discuss, an observation that recalls the idea that one's best activity is to perform well at his craft but not for any purpose. Barth suggests that, after all, all stories are all the same—since ontogeny merely recapitulates."[378] From another perspective, content is a tool to open up fiction to infinite dimensions. From then on, Barth has left behind narrative experimentation, like the one in "Lost in the Funhouse" to achieve a balance between form and content. The balance is the result of his knowledge of great past and present fiction. Barth's works "respond to the discussion in the departments of English and Comparative Literature in his country"[379] as he is an active learned literary figure.

Moreover, Barth's metafictional direction of a balance between form and content has been effective in directing the attention of the literary milieu. Barth's fiction "has become central to interpretation of postmodern literature in general and other 'postmodern' retelling of the *Nights* in particular."[380] In spite of all that, the link between Barth's references to *The Nights* and the development of metafiction has not been appropriately made. For example, "Insufficient attention has been given to the precise nature of Barth's postmodern appreciation of the *Nights*, and his conscious embrace of the Orientalist style of Burton's prose and commentary."[381] The aim of this book, therefore, is to make that link more apparent.

Barth's *Letters* (1979) represents what can be referred to as a relapse in Barth's devotion to *The Nights*. *Letters* reflects Barth's use of another type of referentiality as *Letters* is a self-reflexive novel. Barth, in *Letters*, applies his own theory of innovation in narrative: 'the way forward in narrative is to go backward'; he therefore constructs his novel in the form of letters that contain stories from his previous work. What is obvious in *Letters* is the metafictional property of playfulness in an attempt to stay away from a linear plot.

---

[378] Tharpe 10–11

[379] Hierl 54–5

[380] Parreiras-Horta 139

[381] Parreiras-Horta 139

In the same year, Barth wrote another famous article, "The Literature of Replenishment," where he discusses his vision of experimentation in writing literature; a vision that has developed further since his publication of "The Literature of Exhaustion." In "The Literature of Replenishment," Barth says:

"One certainly does have a sense of having been through this before. Indeed, some of us who have been publishing fiction since the 1950s have had the interesting experience of being praised or damned in that decade as existentialist and in the early 1960s as black humorists. Had our professional careers antedated the Second World War, we would no doubt have been praised or damned as modernists, in the distinguished company listed above. Now we are praised or damned as postmodernists."[382]

Barth's statement shows that change in general is not easy and is always damned until it prevails. Barth reveals the difference he sees between the experimentations of the 1950s and 60s and that of the 1970s as he says: "With varying results, they maintain, postmodernist writers write a fiction that is more and more about itself and its processes, less and less about objective reality and life in the world."[383] This metafictional view in Barth's article reflects his balance between form and content and is supported by his description of his ideal postmodern author or metafictionist in "The Literature of Replenishment" as the one who "neither merely repudiates nor merely imitates either his twentieth-century modernist parents or his nineteenth-century pre-modernist grandparents."[384] The ideal postmodern novel, in Barth's opinion in the same article "will somehow rise above the quarrel between realism and irrealism, formalism and 'contentism,' pure and committed literature, coterie fiction and junk fiction."[385] In Barth's opinion, the ideal postmodern novel is a novel that rises above all of this yet encompasses all of it in order to express personal experience.

In *Tide Water Tales* (1987), reference to *The Nights* is back in Barth's fiction through the character, Shahrazad, but there is also going back to his own fiction, to his novel *Sabbatical* where he borrows characters, themes, spatial and temporal settings. Barth's following work, *The Last Voyage of Somebody the Sailor* (1991), clearly draws on the concepts of the framed story and Sinbad the sailor from *The Nights*. This novel, Hierl thinks, "ingeniously rewrites and expands on *The Nights* to portray the plight of the contemporary postmodern man."[386] This shows that *The Nights* is timeless in conveying personal experience.

Barth's novel, *Once Upon a Time* (1994) and his short story collection, *On With the Story* (1996) are both metafictional in that they stress on the process of story-telling and they both have a frame story. *Once Upon a Time* has the frame story of a sailing trip where the author/narrator tells what seem to be unrelated

---

[382] Barth *Friday Book* 196
[383] Barth *Friday Book* 200
[384] Barth *Friday Book* 203
[385] Barth *Friday Book* 203
[386] Hierl 51

narratives. *On with the Story* discusses story-telling techniques and is self-reflexive in that it draws attention to its fictional nature.

Coming Soon (2001) is also occupied with writing, story-telling, and ambiguity of character/narrator relationships that swing between fiction and reality. *Ten Nights and a Night: Eleven Stories* (2004) follows with the same passion for story-telling, framed narratives, self referentiality, and above all a muse constructed under the shadow of Shahrazad. *Ten Nights* will be fully discussed later on.

Barth's *Where Three Roads Meet* (2005) is a return to Greek mythology. As its main point, the novella has reference to Oedipus and the intersection of the three roads where he learns of his fate; in each of the three stories making the novella, there is the symbol of three roads intersecting for a thematic purpose of the prevalence of faith. In general, Barth's literary trajectory reveals the tremendous amount of literary knowledge, expertise, and talent he has and skillfully uses through his numerous literary fictional and nonfictional works. "Through his academic background and continuous teaching, Barth was able to acquire a literary and philosophical wealth of information that is constantly displayed in his work."[387]

In particular, Barth's occupation and fascination with *The Nights* direct attention to what is there in the atmosphere of this great work. Barth says:

"Its rich dark circumstances, mixing the subtle and the coarse, the comic and the grim, the realistic and the fantastic, the apocalyptic and the hopeful, figure, among other things, both the estate of the fictioneer in general and the particular endeavors and aspirations of this one, at least, who can wish nothing better than to spin like that vizier's excellent daughter, through what nights remain to him, tales within tales within tales, full-stored with 'descriptions and discourse and rare traits and anecdotes and moral instances and reminiscences…proverbs and parables, chronicles and pleasantries, quips and jets, stories and…dialogues and histories and elegies and other verses…'until he and his scribbling are fetched low by the Destroyer of Delights."[388]

This passage shows the richness of *The Nights* as a bottomless source of not only stories that reflect personal experience but also ageless narrative techniques. Barth's fondness for this classic is recently expressed in his work *Ten Nights and a Night: Eleven Stories*.

Of all of Barth's metafictional works, *Ten Nights* is the most important for this book, its discussion of metafiction, and the association this book is making between the original, *The Nights*, and metafiction. A textual analysis of some aspects of Barth's *Ten Nights* will hopefully make this association more apparent. The metafictional elements under discussion include: the syntactic arrangement of the title of the work, and the unique narrative structure of the whole work designed to convey the value of personal experience especially after the international incident of 9/11.

---

[387] Hierl 41

[388] Barth *Friday Book* 59

The syntactic arrangement of the title of *Ten Nights and a Night: Eleven Stories* carries a large load of metafictional connotations. First of all, the inclusion of the word 'night' in the title immediately places this work by Barth into what I propose to be "the art of nights," or "the international cycle of nights." Throughout the ages, literary figures have added their share to the famous story of Shahrazad and Shahrayar through translation and through creation. The numerous translations of this great classic (as translations have become slightly different versions reflective of the cultures that produced each of them) have expanded the cycle of "nights." Translators include Abbe Antone Galland, Andrew Lang, Edward William Lane, John Payne, Richard Burton, J. C. Mardrus, Enno Littmann, Robert Louis Stevenson, N. J. Dawood, Muhsin Mahdi, and Husain Haddawy who have all added some of their personal selves into their translations. The most important literary works that celebrate the art of 'nights' include Edgar Allan Poe's "The Thousand-and-Second Tale of Scheherazade," Jorge Luis Borges' *Seven Nights* and "The Garden of Forking Paths," Naguib Mahfouz's *Arabian Nights and Days*, and Barth's *Ten Nights*. These works are all reflective of "the international cycle of nights." John Barth describes how he felt when he was filing books at Johns Hopkins and losing himself into the tale-cycle by saying:

"One was tacitly permitted to get lost for hours in that splendorous labyrinth and to intoxicate, engorge oneself with *story*. Especially I became enamored of the great tale-cycles and collections: Somadeva's *The Ocean of Story* in ten huge volumes, Burton's *Thousand Nights and a Night* in seventeen, the *Panchatantra*, the *Gesta Romanorum*, the *Novellini* and the *Pent- Hept- and Decameron*. If anything ever makes a writer out of me, it will be the digestion of that enormous, slightly surreptitious feast of narrative."[389]

The most famous of the Oriental cycles is *The Nights*. Barth's whole canon and especially *Ten Nights* shows his appreciation of this amazing construct because it adds two other important elements to the oriental cycle: the metafictional element of 'night' that has continued to dazzle readers and writers over the ages, and the metafictional element of the addition of 'one' to an established number.[390] Barth uses these two elements in the title of *Ten Nights*.

Through these two metafictional elements, and through his choice of title, Barth's *Ten Nights* directs his reader's attention to the 2001/9/11 political attacks on important locations in the United States of America where hundreds of lives were lost. The title, *Ten Nights and a Night*, is loaded with connotations. First, through using the word 'night,'[391] Barth achieves two goals; he is playing with language and its capacity to create new dimensions of meaning through reference to 9/11/2001 (a point to be discussed later)[392]; he is also creating a strong connection between his *Ten Nights* and the original classic, *The Nights*. Third, by adding a number to an established number (ten, a hundred, a thousand etc.),

---

[389] Barth *Friday Book* 57
[390] See above p. 51
[391] See above pp. 70–71
[392] See below p. 120.

Barth also ties his creation to the original classic, and directs his reader's attention to the process of construction of his work in order to problematize the reader's reception of the narrative and its status as real or imaginary. However, the addition of the phrase: *Eleven Stories* to the title further problematizes the reader in receiving the word 'Eleven' as pointing to the real incident that happened in day eleventh of September, or pointing to the number of the imaginary stories (or nights) in the story-collection.

This problematic issue gets a hint of a solution when the narrator of *Ten Nights* starts with, "There was meant to have been a book called *Ten Nights and a Night*, which, had it gotten itself written before TEOTWAW(A)KI 9/11 2001—The End Of The World As We (Americans) Knew It…"[393] Barth, through his narrator, confesses that he had intended to produce *"the hundred-percent-made-up tale…"*[394] with the title: *Ten Nights and a Night* only, i.e. without the word 'Eleven.' But *"He found himself lost…* Paradoxically speaking"[395] due to the catastrophe of 9/11. The reaction of Barth, the metafictionist, was to construct a narrative about the value of fiction in explaining human behavior in general and at times of catastrophe such as the 9/11 attacks in particular. Barth gives his work a title that reflects his intention of creating a metafictional atmosphere similar to that in *The Nights*: a dark gloomy death atmosphere fit for a time following the 9/11 situation of innumerable deaths and probably more deaths if a world war becomes unavoidable as a consequence of the attacks.

Again, like the title of *The Nights*, the title of *Ten Nights* has an additional night that makes a considerable difference in the realm of the realities of the time of the attacks as well as in the realm of fiction. The additional night represents in reality the difference, for Americans, between their world before 9/11 and that after 9/11. Before that date, life was secure, safe, and promising as Americans saw their country as a major power nobody could attack. After that date, Americans have become full of the fear of the ability of others to intrude and turn things around as their country is no longer invincible. In the realm of fiction, the addition of a night to *Ten Nights* creates the same effect achieved in *The Nights*. It creates a form of infinity and continuity for narrative as a construct that expresses personal experience.

The title *Ten Nights and a Night: Eleven Stories*, therefore, has more than one meaning. It indicates reference to the real 9/11 attacks as the work's temporal setting spreads along eleven days and nights following 9/11/2001. This reference is repeated numerous times throughout *Ten Nights* especially in the introductory chapter: "Invocation," and in almost every introduction to the eleven stories.[396] In "Invocation," the extradiegetic narrator says, *"Surely they would have so*

---

[393] Barth *Ten Nights* 1

[394] Barth *Ten Nights* 1

[395] Barth *Ten Nights* 1

[396] Quotations represented are of fragmented nature due to Barth's highly fragmented style of writing, and fragmentation is a metafictional property. But, Barth in *Ten Nights* is over-using fragmentation to an extent only he (with his long literary career) can get away with

gotten, well ere now, had not shit hit the world-in-general's fan, and the US of A's in particular; on that certain September morn, killing thousands of innocents and, just possibly, American Innocence itself."[397] In the introduction to the first story, Graybard the narrator says, "All which implies that—shit having hit fan and the World As We'd Known It having effectively ended on Nine eleven O One—said book cannot now so open?"[398] In the introduction to the second story, there is a reference to "Black Tuesday, 2001."[399] Page 41 of *Ten Nights* has the extradiegetic narrator saying, "She'd heard on the car radio that hijacked airliners were crashing into New York's World Trade Center towers and the Pentagon, maybe even the White House and the Capital." Page 65 has Osama (Ibn Laden) as the one behind the 9/11 attacks.[400]

The title, *Ten Nights and a Night: Eleven Stories* provides the possibility of yet another meaning as the work encompasses eleven stories, ten of which were separately published before from 1960 to 2001. Barth adds a story that had not been published before to give infinity to his title and achieve the double meaning. However, Barth has chosen these eleven stories to be included in *Ten Nights* even though he probably has other uncollected stories. It seems he has chosen these eleven stories to be included under the title *Ten Nights* for their relevance to meanings he intends to convey in *Ten Nights*. Most of these stories have a negative depressed attitude fit for the time of the production of *Ten Nights*. Barth's narrator sarcastically and playfully says about the choice of stories in *Ten Nights,*

"Most of them Autumnal, shall we say, in theme and tone, addressing such jolly topics as the approach of old age, declining capabilities, and death—but a couple not. And several having to do, for better or worse, with (hang on your hats, folks)...the Telling of Stories!"[401]

These types of gloomy atmospheres usually hang over heads when people are faced with a situation of death they cannot cope with or seemed unable to explain. Likewise, it is well-established that stories and tales in *The Nights* were circulating folktales known before they were included in that famous book. They have probably been chosen from among many other folktales for their relevance to the situation of Shahrayar and Shahrazad.

Right from the start, it appears that the whole of *Ten Nights* is metafictional. The very title is reference to reality, through bringing forward the world before

---

[397] Barth *Ten Nights* 3–4

[398] Barth *Ten Nights* 19

[399] Barth *Ten Nights* 31

[400] More and more references of the sort are in *Ten Nights*: the introduction to the fourth story opens with, "Friday, September 14, 2001 in Hendecameronland" (Ten Nights 85). Page 111, has reference to Al Qaeda terrorists. References to the real incident of 9/11/2001 go on and on until the last chapter titled, "Afterwords [sic]," which has, "All which reminds one that in Shakespeare, as in most art and no small measure of life, what you see, at first glance at least, is not what you get. But this present Twelfth Night eve, we were saying: Sept Twenty-two O One, the Neverlasting now..." (*Ten Nights* 295)

[401] Barth *Ten Nights* 3

and after the 9/11 attacks, and to fiction through an analogy with the title of *The Nights*. But in *Ten Nights* Barth imitates not only *The Nights* but also several other classical fictions: Boccaccio's *Decameron*, what he referred to as Marguerite of Navarre's *Heptameron* and Giovanni Battista Basile's Pentameron[402] in order to give his own version of reality. In addition to this, Barth's preoccupation with the process of narration through his explicit story-telling techniques reveals his metafictional style of balancing form and content as metafiction is represented in "its direct and immediate concern with fiction-making itself."[403] Barth is probably one of a few metafictionists who are still insisting on the intricate style of referentiality mixed with the narrative technique of writing fiction through the discussion of the process of narration between narrator and reader or between narrator and muse.

The unique structure of Barth's *Ten Nights* reflects his vision of fiction and the purposes it serves. *Ten Nights* is a collection of eleven separate stories, but it has introductions to these stories which make the work appear as a cohesive whole. Through this structure, the narrator puts forward three important narrative issues outlined in "Invocation," the introduction to the first night story. The first narrative issue stresses the importance of the nature of the relationship between an author and his source of inspiration. The second narrative issue defines the nature of 'story' itself. The third narrative issue proposes a renewal or modernization of relationship between man and woman in general and male and female in literature.

In order to discuss these three narrative issues, Barth's 2004 book is structured around a frame narrative that encompasses eleven main narratives plus other narratives such as an additional experimental four-page narrative, "Help," which is not really a story but what Barth refers to as "a stereophonic narrative for authorial voice,"[404] where Barth repeatedly calls for help! However, *Ten Nights* does not start right away with the first-night story but with a narrative piece; an introduction titled 'Invocation' where the relationship between the extradiegetic narrator, the intradiegetic narrator, and the muse, the source of inspiration, is illuminated to reveal the first narrative issue of the relationship between an author/narrator and his muse. This type of introduction precedes each and every night story in *Ten Nights* and it takes a form of conversation between the narrator and his muse. 'Invocation,' the first introduction, starts with,

"*There was meant to have been a book* called *Ten Nights and a Night*, which, had it gotten itself written before TEOTWAW(A)KI 9/11 2001—The End Of The World As We (Americans) Knew It"—might have opened with a sportive extended invocation to the Storyteller's Muse, more or less like this,

---

[402] Barth *Ten Nights* 3
[403] Christensen 10
[404] Barth *Ten Nights* 10–13

"Tell, O Muse of Story, the hundred-percent-made-up tale of a modern-day Odysseus's interlude with the brackish tidewater march-nymph here called WYSIWYG—"[405]

The beginning with this introductory invocation is important for two reasons. First, it represents an act of calling the narrative effect of Odysseus's interlude (one of the first narratives according to Western standards) to reappear at our present time. Barth's *Ten Nights* does not exactly fight death but it rather displays the author's own understanding, through narrative, of circumstances that have led to it. Second, the inclusion of "Tell, o muse of a story," shows Barth's first narrative priority which is the relationship with the muse. This reference to epic technique is enhanced in the introductory paragraph in *Ten Nights* with the mention of the epic hero, Odysseus, most famous for the return home journey of ten years (there are possible connotations of the number ten) he made after the Trojan War. The inclusion of references to *The Odyssey* and *The Iliad* in the first paragraph in *Ten Nights* shows Barth's insistence on his metafictional referentiality to human experiences in classical fiction.

Within "Invocation," the first introduction, language play in the form of acronyms is another metafictional element of structure in *Ten Nights*; an element that also strengthens the first narrative issue of the relationship between author/narrator and muse to look at different aspects of human experience. Barth uses internet jargon as the name of the muse in his work: 'WYSIWYG' (What You See Is What You Get). Barth's use of this name ironically points to element of fate. Barth says, "Irony, is the clear consciousness of eternal agility, of an infinitely teeming chaos."[406] To verify the choice of this ironical acronym, Barth's extradiegetic narrator is lost to the extent of giving such a weird name of a muse. He says:

How, in an advanced but still-healthy decade of his sleeping and waking, breathing air and pumping blood, eating/drinking/pissing/shitting, learning and teaching, dressing and undressing…All in Miz Muse's good time. He found himself lost— (*Ten Nights* 1)

The reason behind the feeling of loss is that the Western man was going on with his daily routines, and suddenly everything changed. The change was so drastic that it marked, according to Barth, 'TEOTWAW(A)KI' (The End Of The World As We (Americans) Knew It), which is another ironical acronym. In an attempt to trace an inspirational source for Barth's use of acronyms, it helps to go back to another work inspired by *The Nights*. It is Edgar Allan Poe's short story, "The Thousand and Second Tale of Scheherazade," where he uses an acronym saying: "Having had occasions, lately, in the course of some oriental

---

[405] Barth *Ten Nights* 1.This quotation appears and reappears in this book because Barth opens his collection with it, it carries loads of metafictional connotations, and it represents an excellent piece of literature that concentrates on the value of narratives, real or imaginary, in the face of disaster.

[406] Barth *Further Fridays* 320

investigation, to consult the 'tellmenow Isitsoornot', a work which…is scarcely known at all, even in Europe."[407] The discussion of Poe's style of writing and metafiction has been included in the previous chapter, but his use of this acronym, in particular, is a clear example of his creativity and affiliation with *The Nights* represented in his concern about the fate of Shahrazad at the end of those nights. Poe's short story reveals two points of precedence in the West: the first is the use of an acronym, and the second is the discussion of the process of writing within the body of a fictional work as has been revealed in the quote from Poe's short story. Barth's use of acronyms in *Ten Nights*_displays a strong possibility that he was affected by Poe's fictional creativity, especially in "The Thousand and Second Tale of Scheherazade." *Ten Nights* also reveals that Barth was affected by another contemporary metafictional work, *Arabian Nights and Days*, by the Egyptian Nobel Prize winner Naguib Mahfouz.[408]

In addition, Poe's short story, *The Nights*, and metafiction have some form of link to the concept of arabesque which is apparent in Poe's work *Tales of the Grotesque and Arabesque* and in Barth's *Ten Nights*. The acronyms in *Ten Nights* are arabesque in that they are intricate verbal expressions that carry connotations of the wondrous and unnatural. Barth explains the concept of arabesque by saying:

It is centered on the playful treatment of artistic form…the discussion of the work or form or medium along with the actual object of portrayal; and, indeed, in the extreme instances, the portraying of the form or the medium *instead* of the object… The arabesque involves the rupture of illusion by references in the text to its author, to the process of writing, and so forth; the transgression of the boundary between the reality of reader and author and the reality of the characters and world of the text; the privileging of the interplay between and among norms, forms, voices, themes, and languages.[409]

Through exploration of the concept of arabesque, which in definition very much resembles metafiction, and the exploration of *The Nights*, which Barth asserts cannot be exhausted,[410] Barth has created the frame narrative of *Ten Nights*. In this work, Barth mixes the art of fiction with the process of writing fiction in a highly intricate and metafictional manner. This manner is present, to a large degree, in his distinctive linguistic style accompanied by his vast knowledge of literary works from the past and the present.

The frame narrative of *Ten Nights*, with all its political, social, and historic connotations, is constructed around an authoritative male writer, Graybard, who appears to be the imagination of the extradiegetic narrator. The name Graybard is an interesting name as it is a coinage of two words, gray and bard. Both parts of the word refer to Barth's long-life occupation with fiction and seeing himself a bard like Shakespeare and other epic bards. Graybard narrates stories and

---

[407] Edgar Allan Poe 507

[408] On page 113, there are references to works built upon or associated with the original, *The Nights*.

[409] Barth *Further Fridays* 321

[410] Barth *Further Fridays* 289

exchanges conversations with a female (muse) named WYSIWYG (What You See Is What You Get), which is internet language. Both characters exchange conversations and narrate stories during eleven nights and refrain from narration when daytime arrives in another obvious correlation to *The Nights*. What is significant is that these eleven nights start following the Sept. 11, 2001 attacks on USA when Americans there were greatly affected.

The male character, Graybard, and the female character muse, WYSIWYG, spend eleven nights together, sleeping together, making fun of the world, and narrating stories. This framework, which is a response to the present as well as a recall of past literary classics, is Barth's way of viewing the relationship between an author/narrator and his muse; it is also the author's search for truth which is no longer obtained from science or from logic.

For Barth, it is Western science and philosophy that is guilty of falsification and obfuscation in attempting to impose concepts of time, logic, and grammar upon a fluid 'reality' better grasped by Eastern mysticism and The Arabian Nights.'[411]

Greek and Oriental mythology in general and *The Nights* in particular have been for Barth points of departure and sources of inspiration for his metafictional novel, *Ten Nights* intended to explore personal experience.

To counteract Western logic and order, Barth chooses the chaos of metafiction as a better tool fit for today's age, and he, the fictionist and literary critic, has been exploiting the dimensions of metafiction throughout his development as a fictionist. In the 1960s, in *Lost in the Funhouse*, Barth mixes between fiction and the straightforward process of writing fiction creating a recognizable metafictional text. Nevertheless, he gave that up, and in 2004, he instead mixes between fiction and the almost unlimited metafictional opportunities of writing he has, to the extent of explicitly including not only the process of writing fiction but also his relationship with his muse. In addition, he includes his reasons for writing fiction inside his fictional work. Barth here is a novelist who "has a message to convey and is not merely displaying his technical brilliance."[412] Barth explains his first purpose in writing *Ten Nights*, which is

"To put these originally unrelated tales into a narrative frame, connecting their dots to make a whole somewhat larger (and perhaps a bit friskier) than the mere sum of its parts, as in such exemplary instances as *The Book of a Thousand Nights and a Night*; also Boccaccio's *Decameron*, Marguerite of Navarre's *Heptameron*, Giovanni Battista Basile's *Pentameron*, and other *such-amerons*..."[413]

Then WYSIWYG, the muse, comments, "In a word, a Hendecamerons?"[414] Her remark probably means a combination of Eastern and Western narrative canons. Graybard agrees with her and adds his second purpose as the present Teller "thus clearing the narrative decks, so to speak, to recharge and reorient

---

[411] Parreiras-Horta 141–142

[412] Christensen 11

[413] Barth *Ten Nights* 3

[414] Barth *Ten Nights* 3

their original author's imagination. Whom never mind,"[415] he says. Regardless of Barth's intentions of placing his fiction and himself as a fictionist among or in parallel with world's classics, his own words reveal his metafictional direction backward not to the 1960s metafictional abstract experimentations, but much farther towards Hend (India), the thought origin of the frame narrative cycles, and especially to *The Nights* for means of expression.

In *Ten Nights*, as in the case of its predecessors especially *The Nights*, it is not only the individual stories but also the frame narrative and structure that provide *Ten Nights* with significance. Throughout these eleven nights, the two lovers exchange stories, a story each night with a type of playful conversational introductions. These introductions serve as networks paving the way for the coming of each story, serving as links that tie these eleven stories together, and taking *Ten Nights* away from being a mere collection of short stories to be more like a unified culturally and historically oriented text. More importantly, these introductions clarify Barth's first narrative issue in *Ten Nights*, which is the nature of the relationship between author/narrator and muse.

Barth's extradiegetic narrator affirms this long relationship in the introduction to the first night story by saying: "Night One of their reconnection and Extended Congress may be young; her present company isn't."[416] The relationship between a writer and his muse is always as old as the writing career of that writer, and in the case of Barth, it is about sixty plus years. The introduction to the first night story of *Ten Nights* introduces the first night story, which, according to Barth, is "meant to illustrate not so much that art may be a cry for help as that Distress, like any other emotion, circumstance, or what have you, may be grist for Ms. Muse's mill. Shall they grind on?"[417] The discussion of the relationship between a writer and his muse inside fiction is an example of fiction about fiction making, which is clearly metafictional.

The imaginary detailed sort of relationship between the intradiegetic narrator, Graybard, and the muse WYSIWYG continues throughout the eleven introductions in *Ten Nights*. Graybard, the intradiegetic narrator, and the extradiegetic narrator constantly address their reader while discussing the process of construction of this book and of narration in general. However, all of this seems trivial as the news and live pictures of the 9/11 experience dominate all scenes. Nevertheless, conversations between Graybard, imagination, and his muse, inspiration, become resources for the completion for the same process of narration. WYSIWYG comments on this by saying: "It worked for Scheherazade, and it'll work for us. Because inspiration's the name of the game, right? It's who and what I freaking *am!* Or at least its Serviceable Surrogate."[418] Graybard comments: "But I have a thousand and one questions, Wys." His questions to her include who she really is and where they both are. He does not wait for her answers, and he answers that they both are not in the world of reality

---

[415] Barth *Ten Nights* 3
[416] Barth *Ten Nights* 18
[417] Barth *Ten Nights* 18
[418] Barth *Ten Nights* 44

by saying: "You're the physical embodiment of every yarn-spinner's indispensable collaborator, materialized here in a march-country version of Mount Parnassus—"[419] In just a short passage, there are obvious references to *The Nights* in his questions to her, and to Greek mythology in the mention of Mount Parnassus where the muses lived. Such references expand the scope of *Ten Nights* to include realities such as the 9/11 facts and fictions in references to past world classics. In addition, throughout introductions to stories, the conversations of Graybard and his muse keep reminding the reader of the process of writing fiction in a metafictional attempt to connect bits and pieces of *Ten Nights* to become a unified whole in an obvious reference to the nature of the relationship between narrator and muse.

In the process of fiction making, pursuing a muse is a difficult task, a point included in *Ten Nights* in the discussion of the relationship between narrator and muse. The extradiegetic narrator explains how Graybard prepares himself for writing, for inspiration, but she, his muse, is not willing to come forward.

Yo, Wys? He called… No reply. Well, he'd wait a bit and just see. The woman might of course have other business than attending to his inspiration; perhaps even (twinge of jealousy here) other imaginations than his to inspire in her singular and delightsome fashion.[420]

Graybard prepares himself for her coming, but there is no luck; a typical situation of the difficulty of a writer's pursuit of inspiration. Barth continues this metafictional discussion of the process of writing within his fiction with the extradiegetic narrator, saying:

"Having delivered himself of his soliloquy [the above concern of the muse not coming], he deposited Ultimatum #4 in the empty wineglass and unhurriedly shucked his clothes…tossed them among and atop hers, and took his narratorial ease on the glowing waterbed, stretching himself out neither on His side thereof nor on Hers, but straight down the middle. As if cued by his open-ended resolve, all the room-lights dimmed as one and then went out entirely. The simple symbolism pleased him, as had that of his and her clothing in damp bedside congress: In the imminence of their muse, even seasoned practitioners of any art are finally naked and in the dark, waiting (with honed attention) to see what will happen next."[421]

The above quotations are just examples of the many such passages of the relationship between narrators and muse in *Ten Nights*, which is over burdened with the process of narration than with narration itself even though the relationship is displayed in narrative-like situations. It is ironic to mention that these lengthy passages in *Ten Nights* serve the purpose of the, "I heard O happy king that…" repeated by Shahrazad in the beginning of the story that starts each of *The Nights*.

Speculation over narration continues throughout introductions to stories between Graybard the imagination and WYSIWYG the inspiration while

---

[419] Barth *Ten Nights* 4
[420] Barth *Ten Nights* 141
[421] Barth *Ten Nights* 144

including the metafictional element of mixing facts with fiction; mixing the political situation of the few days following the 9/11 attacks within the fictional world of *Ten Nights*. Barth calls his narrative progress "reviewing the inventory,"[422] or looking back to what has been finished of this work. The extradiegetic narrator says that Graybard remarked…"that whereas that old bit called *Help!*, back at Invocation-time, had been truly a fiction but not truly a story, Third Night's *Ring* and Fourth's *Dead Cat* had been truly stories but not truly fictions, they being more-true-than-not Reasonably Recent productions both. The intervening item (First Night's *Landscape*) had been truly both Fiction and Story, but by no means Reasonably Recent…Muse willing, the remaining items would all be all three—cross his heart and excuse the *goyishe* expression. Seven to go, is it?"[423]

It is obvious from this that *Ten Night* is equally occupied with the process of writing fiction when writing fiction. The above statement also reveals how far Barth is able to go on breaking the narrative rules prevailing before the onset of metafiction.

The second narrative issue Barth discusses in his introductions is the nature of a story. A story, according to Barth, does not necessarily become a story for having a beginning, middle, and end. It is built "through sequential escalations to a sort of climax and resolution."[424] This issue asserts Barth's occupation with metafictional narrative techniques, as he believes they are more appropriate for this contemporary age of political instability. Discussing this issue, Barth includes the reader and what s/he might think while reading, "Reader him/herself might be interested to know that this pair [Graybard and WYSIWYG] are commencing Night Three of their project-more-or-less-in-progress after all."[425] Barth's style of writing *Ten Nights*, especially in the introductions to stories, is in fact over burdened with the process of narration than with narration itself in passages such as:

"Done, more or less—always bearing in mind that Less can be more. It's another riff on both our Totally Innocent Et Cetera theme and on images whose narrative exploitation neither exhausts nor exorcises them."[426]

From a metafictional narrative view, therefore, the title and introductions to stories in *Ten Nights* are more important than the individual stories that make up much of the bulk of *Ten Nights* especially when discussing the first and second narrative issues of the relationship between narrators and muse and the nature of story. However, the second narrative issue of the nature of a story is also a theme depicted from the inclusion of the eleven stories into *Ten Nights*. Regardless of the meaning of a story in isolation, its meaning would be different when placed within a certain spatial or temporal context. These eleven stories acquire new meanings when included in the politically and socially oriented *Ten Nights*.

---

[422] Barth *Ten Nights* 88
[423] Barth *Ten Nights* 88
[424] Barth *Ten Nights* 18
[425] Barth *Ten Nights* 63
[426] Barth *Ten Nights* 70

"Landscape: The Eastern Shore," the first night's story in *Ten Nights*, published in 1961, acquires new meaning forty years after its initial publication. Unlike the 9/11 sudden unexpected deaths of old and young victims, the protagonist, Captain Claude Morgan is an aging man spending what is left of his life contemplating life and living experiences, and expecting death quietly and peacefully as he has taken his chance and lived his youth.

"It will not occur to him to make the effort to move his joint-bones, one against the other, to carry himself downstairs so that he might stoke butter beans into his stomach in order to lift himself back into this room and place his body upon this chair, where it rests at present from living years that stretch behind him like a taut dredge-rope."[427]

This image of the difficulties of movements in old age counteracts the vigor of those who died young during the 9/11 attacks. There is a big difference between the ends of the lives of people who were killed in 9/11 and between the life of Captain Claude Morgan who has had his share of living and is patiently waiting for life to end. From the inclusion of this story into *Ten Nights*, Barth aims at concentrating on the second narrative issue of the nature of a story.

A story could be equally valuable to carry experience regardless of subject matter. It could be dealing with a grand narrative such as faith, resurrection, death, after life, or it could be dealing with a trivial everyday aspect of living. In both situations, a story is enjoyable because of its aesthetic value. "The Ring" is about a character finding a ring in a sea while on holiday and trying to find out the owner of that ring. The whole concept of when the ring was lost, to whom it belongs, and why it is in the sea creates stories upon stories. These speculations in "The Ring" reveal how stories are formed or take place, which bring into mind the second narrative issue in Barth's introduction to the first story in *Ten Nights*, which is the nature of a story. This is probably one reason why "The Ring" is included in *Ten Nights*.

Also, the explored idea of 'rings' in literature in "The Ring" gives further significance to this story and a second reason for it to find a place in *Ten Nights*. The narrator mentions

"Plato's Gygean ring of invisibility, a thought-experiment for testing true virtue; jealous Hans Carvel's fabliau dream-ring; Browning's *The Ring and the Book*; Tolkien's *Lord of the Rings*; several magical rings in *The Thousand and One Nights*; and other material rings such as tree rings, key rings, earrings, nose and nipple rings, annular eclipses, ring nebulae etc."[428]

This juxtaposition of the mention of rings in great works of art and in ordinary everyday linguistic expressions illuminates the metafictional tendencies of mixing high and low living.

The story "A Detective and a Turtle" acquires its place in *Ten Nights* again because of the subject of life-giving story-telling. Story-telling here is a tool to look back at the recent history of the United States and how it went from being a super power to being a target for attack. This position becomes apparent only

---

[427] Barth *Ten Nights* 27
[428] Barth *Ten Nights* 53

after the 9/11 attacks. The extradiegetic narrator says: "So went their decades, zip-zip-zip, of life's short story: in the Mason's [the protagonists] case, the twentieth century's latter half, during which, so it seems to them, American decades lost their former flavor."[429] With the loss of former flavor, the extradiegetic narrator contemplates on the whole process of writing fiction and its usefulness. The slow pace of inspiration is not the only concern for a writer. The experience of spending long hours writing fiction, then not being able to sell what has been written, is equally frustrating.

Barth's exploration of the nature of a story continues with "The Rest of Your Life," which starts with, "SOUNDS LIKE THE BEGINNING OF A STORY."[430] Repeated a second time in the next page, this sentence directs attention to the nature of a story through its process of story-telling, and to the relevance of its subject matter to *Ten Nights* as a whole. "The Rest of Your Life" tells of a computer error taking the protagonist back to a day in 1956. That period in American history was characterized by optimism and hope of a good future even though new technologies associated with computer science were not as sophisticated as they had become in 2004. This story also gains its place in *Ten Nights* for its implied connotations associated with that period in contrast to the present.

In "The Big Shrink," Barth uses a well-known scientific theory of the expansion then shrinking of the universe to metafictionally refer to reality and to fiction at the same time: to the political situation of the declining power of the United States of America, and to his own declining ability of writing fiction. Fred Mackall, the protagonist says that "the universe isn't expanding anymore the way it used to."[431] A few paragraphs down, the author explores the idea of aging and loss of vigor and artistic abilities when his protagonist says:

"Fifty, Fifty-five, I'd say. Sixty tops. Then things sort of stalled for the next five or so, and after that the volume of space held steadily, but your galaxies and stars and such actually began to shrink, at an ever-increasing clip, and they're shrinking still."[432]

The story "Extension" seems to be, in its themes, an extension of "The Big Shrink." As Barth says in the latter story: "They say that the universe itself is extending; seems to me the case could be made that for some time now it's been holding still at best, while we ourselves have begun to shrink."[433] Barth asserts in the same story that "For us, the theme of the season and no doubt of all seasons to come was not Extension, but Contraction."[434] "Extension" ends by the protagonist sitting with his wife "like ticketed passengers in an airport

---

[429] Barth *Ten Nights* 93–4
[430] Barth *Ten Nights* 116
[431] Barth *Ten Nights* 145
[432] Barth *Ten Nights* 146
[433] Barth *Ten Nights* 172
[434] Barth *Ten Nights* 171

lounge,"[435] weak with age, waiting to leave the atmospheres of things familiar to them.

The story "9999" explores another facet of the nature of story. A recurring theme might grant a story such as "9999" a position in a collection such as *Ten Nights*. This story reveals Barth's fascination with numbers and their significance. In the story, the protagonist and other characters who are members of the same family were born on dates with the numbers nine and/or eleven. Interactions among the characters hint that 9/11 is meant to be; it is an indication of fate, which is a refutation of Western science and logic.

The third narrative issue in *Ten Nights* is that Barth is proposing a renewal, a modernization of the relationship between man and woman in general and a modernization of already existing narrative situations. This narrative issue appears in the introductions to stories and also in some stories. Barth's narrator calls it "a change of agenda after all, from Shiva's-and-Parvati's or Scheherazade's-and-Shahryar's to Graybard's-and-Wysiwyg's."[436] In all introductions to stories, inspiration is a woman not forced to come with narratives when situations call for them, like Shahrazad of *The Nights*, but rather an independent woman who comes at her own pace. The strength of a woman is apparent in the story "And Then There's the One" where the granddaughter of the protagonist (in reference to contemporary young women) announces she is not going to bear a child. Her decision is seen, in this story, to cause a decline in Western populations paving the way for other non-Western fertile nations to dominate. In the eyes of the narrator, a man, the freedom and independence women get are possible causes for population imbalance that might lead to weakness and wars! This is probably the reason for this story's existence in *Ten Nights*. On the other hand, this freedom and independence of women who are sources of inspiration are concerns for aging authors unable to attract inspiration easily. This situation is a call for despair delivered in Barth's complicated style of writing:

"Just now he feels bearing of that massive inverted pyramid—of which he and his beloved Betsy and each of all the rest of us is individually the vertex— as if it were an enormous hydraulic press, and dear sunny Granddaughter Donna its all-too-human diamond point. Forget it, Reader. Brother! Sister! Daughter! Son! Forget it."[437]

Barth's repeated calls to his reader's attention at the closure of "And There's the One" is a metafictional tool in *Ten Nights*.

In *Ten Nights*, there are several stories that have all the three narrative issues Barth outlined in the first introduction. "Dead Cat, Floating Boy," "Click," and "WYSIWYG?" explore the nature of the author/muse relationship, the nature of story, and the renewal of the relationship between man and woman. "Dead Cat, Floating Boy," shows Barth's constant exploration of all three narrative issues in art and in reality. In the story, a man writer, referred to as 'Narrator,' in an

---

[435] Barth *Ten Nights* 172
[436] Barth *Ten Nights* 19
[437] Barth *Ten Nights* 196–7

obvious self-conscious relation to narration and consequently to his inspiration or muse, meets a woman, half his age, coming to his doorstep to tell him about a dead cat. She is concerned about the dead cat while he is attracted to her youth and liveliness; these are aspects he no longer possesses. Aging authors strive for young inspirations, which are hard to get. The second half of the story is a narrative about an autistic boy of ten who escapes death even though he was missing for four days while swimming in a swamp. Again, the phenomenon of death or escaping death colors this story and makes it fit for *Ten Nights* especially when Barth includes historic and mythical survivors from all over the world, such as Prophet Moses, baby Perseus, baby Oedipus, the Yavapai-Apache Prophet's daughter, Odysseus, and Sinbad.[438] In another reference to art and life, Barth asserts that all of us are "floating through our life-stories like unread messages in bottles or galaxies in the void, and into dream-country every mortal night."[439]

The story "Click" also explores these three narrative issues. A man, Fred, and a woman, Irma, interact online while working on their PCs in the manner of a modern relationship between man and woman. The extradiegetic narrator makes too many metafictional deviations from his story to strengthen his relationship with his reader. "Click" explicitly goes into the concept of hyper-textuality visible in the text through capital letters, underlined words, bracketed words, anagrams, pastiche expressions, etc. Implicitly, "Click" hints at the value of the content of a story or the experiences it contains at a certain time or another. Ironically, "Click" was written when computer science was at a certain point of advancement. Time passes and technology advances leaving behind what seemed very scientific in the near past. Barth's reason for including "Click" in *Ten Nights* is probably to show that an interesting story at a time becomes trivial when time surpasses it with other kinds of knowledge.

The story, "WYSIWYG?" is the only story published for the first time, and it serves as a closure for *Ten Nights*. WYSIWYG is the muse and major character who interacts with the narrator in story-telling in *Ten Nights*. Their interactions make the backbone of this work, define the nature of stories included, and explore the intimate relationship between man and woman. In the introduction to this story, Graybard says:

"All I wanted, all we needed, was a bit of a frame-tale to connect those eleven miscellaneous items and make them into a *book* instead of a mere collection, right? So we come up with this wacko Wysiwyg/Muse/Imaginarium idea and decide to give it a spin, see whether it'll fly, never mind the mixed metaphor— but then *wham!* Along comes Nine Eleven, and suddenly it's a whole nasty new world out there, and how're we supposed to float a butcher's dozen irrelevant stories about Autumnality and Innocent Marital Guilt and Stuck Storytellers et cet., now that big-time shit has hit the national fan and Apocalypse has moved in just around the corner?"[440]

---

[438] Barth *Ten Nights* 75
[439] Barth *Ten Nights* 75–76
[440] Barth *Ten Nights* 264

It is the contemporary age of metafiction with all its open dimensions that allows authors to be as informal as they please. Barth here displays his intentions and his craft right in the open, and "WYSIWYG," the story, looks more like the introductions to stories in *Ten Nights* rather than a story itself. Barth asserts the nature of his imaginary muse:

"By no means, but never mind. This march, Reader, this night, this moon, these tides, are real…and tyrannies of every sort, not to mention that catastrophic final gift of the Terrible Twentieth to the Terrifying Twenty-first, the literal global plaque of AIDS. All real. But this glassy Imaginarium is, well, imaginary—Q.E.D a few pages past."[441]

In rounding off his work (with the narrator, the muse, and the process of writing he had started with), Barth is insisting on displaying his style of writing fiction through the inclusion of metafictional elements either in each story or in the introduction to each of these stories. The metafictional elements in any work "scrutinize all facets of the literary construct—language, the conventions of plot and character, the relation of the artists to his art and to his reader."[442] From another perspective, metafiction "takes as its main subject writers, writing, and anything else which has to do with the way books and stories are written."[443] Is Barth's *Ten Nights* capable of exploring the relations between the writer and his written text? In other words, has Barth been successful in conveying the value of personal experience partially by replacing fiction with the technique of writing fiction? The answer is left to each reader's view of fiction and pleasure derived from reading fiction, but there is one thing for sure. Barth has structured *Ten Nights* in rather small narrative units very similar to units in *The Nights*. He did this in order to arrive at a system that functions as a whole construct. As described above, the metafictional elements in this work have a strong analogy with the metafictional elements in *The Nights*. In addition, Barth has packed his work with a wide range of fictional and non-fictional historical references and allusions in an attempt to open up his text for interpretation. That way, each reader would have a chance to construct his own world of fiction. Barth explains how he arranges his fiction by saying:

"At heart I'm an arranger still, whose chiefest literary pleasure is to take a received melody—an old narrative poem, a classical myth, a shopworn literary convention, a shard of my experience, a *New York Times* Book Review series— and, improvising like a jazzman within its constraints, reorchestrate it to present purpose."[444]

In Barth's fiction, therefore, there is a specific pattern that can be followed. In his intertextual references to other narratives, Barth often mixes Western references, usually Greek mythology, with Eastern references, *The Nights, Katha Sarit Sagara, The Panchatantra* etc. In Barth's article, "Muse, Spare Me," he uses Greek mythology as his metafictional reference, and then he ends in the

---

[441] Barth *Ten Nights* 273
[442] Christensen 10
[443] McCaffery "The Art of Metafiction" 22
[444] Barth *Friday Book* 7

same article with a metafictional reference to Shahrazad of *The Nights*. Barth justifies his fondness for Shahrazad by referring to the frame-story of the Nights:

"Though the tales she tells aren't my favorite, she remains my favorite teller, and it is a heady paradox that this persistence, being the figure of her literal aim, thereby generates itself, and becomes the emblem as well of my hope, musewise, in the time between now and when I shall run out of ink or otherwise expire, it is Scheherazade who comes to mind, for many reasons—not least of which is a technical interest in the ancient device of the framing-story, used more beautifully in the *Nights* than anywhere else I know."[445]

In "Muse, Spare Me," it seems that Barth is apologizing for his use of the Eastern classic, *The Nights*, through two moves. First, he relates his admiration for Shahrazad to the ancient device of the frame-story which existed before *The Nights*. Second, he accompanies that Eastern reference with a Western reference to Greek mythology. Barth's novella, "Dunyazadiad" (1972), also shows his pattern of reference to Western mythology, represented in the suffix –iad added to the title, which is also the name of Shahrazad's sister. Implicitly, the formation of the title, "Dunyazadiad," is an example of how the major work, *The Nights*, has been acculturated in the West. In her book, *Nocturnal Poetics: The Arabian Nights in Comparative Context*, Ferial Ghazoul goes on to compare how *The Nights* has been received by two prominent authors, John Barth and Jorge Luis Borges. She says:

"Barth *appreciates* the work of the Other and uses their structures, plots, and themes to present the Self. Borges *joins* the works of the Other, seeing the concerns of the Self in them. Barth annexes the Other while Borges unites with the Other. There is a kind of violent possession in Barth's treatment of *The Arabian Nights* while Borges submits almost mystically to its matrix."[446]

Barth appreciates *The Nights* by recognizing 'the art of nights,' by using names of characters from this classic such as Shahrazad, Duniazad itc., and by celebrating the device of the framing story. However, Barth's appreciation of *The Nights* has almost always been accompanied by a reference or references to Greek mythologies. For example, the addition of the suffix –iad in Barth's title, "Dunyazadiad," reveals, according to Ghazoul, that "the Eastern has been turned morphologically into something classical; i.e., Greek and Latin."[447] It is Barth's intention to domesticate *The Nights*. He has been intentionally using *The Night* "to emphasize his own presence in the text and to draw attention to the Self and away from the Other."[448] In other words, Barth has been using techniques of metafiction differently than, say, Borges or Mahfouz.[449]

---

[445] Barth *Friday Book* 57

[446] Ghazoul *Nocturnal Poetics* 123

[447] Ghazoul *Nocturnal Poetics* 123

[448] Ghazoul *Nocturnal Poetics* 127

[449] Ferial J. Ghazoul, in her book *Nocturnal Poetics: The Arabian Nights in Comparative Context*, compares the treatment of *The Nights* of Borges and Barth. Ghazoul says: "In studying the use of the Arabian tales by Borges and Barth and their modes of

Barth's *Ten Nights* also shows his pattern of mixing Eastern and Western references to create his own world of fiction; a world that ironically and intentionally shows the intellectual superiority of the West. Although Barth's pattern of the mixture of self-reflexivity between *The Nights* and Greek mythology has not changed during the course of his writing career, his attitude towards reality infused in fiction is what has changed. Several factors contribute to this change. The publication of Edward Said's polemic book, *Orientalism* (1978), the application of the notions of Chaos Theory in literature, and the translation of other literary works dealing with *The Nights*, Mahfouz's *Arabian Nights and Days* (to be discussed in the next chapter) have led to the change in John Barth's metafictional strategies, especially his depiction of reality in his treatment of *The Nights* in particular. These three factors, which will be briefly discussed respectively, have been effective not only in changing Barth's fiction but also in changing the trajectory of metafiction and literary theory.

Although Said's *Orientalism* is a book of cultural studies, it has been tremendously useful in literary criticism especially in the interpretation of the reception of translated Oriental works such as *The Nights*. For example, according to Said, everything the Orientals said and did was recorded irrespective of its context, and projected to the civilized world of the West. Translations of *The Nights*, therefore, provided for Westerners what was thought to be correct images of the Orient. Richard Burton's translation, in particular, projects an exotic erotic magical world that has nothing to do with reality. Parreiras-Horta says that Burton aims at

"an idiosyncratic anthropology of alternative sexual practices of East and West. Burton's emendations to the tale of 'Qamar al-Zaman and Prince Boudour,' in particular, stress on acceptance of homosexuality and blurring of gender roles in a manner which would appeal to twentieth-century writers."[450]

Barth's insistence on the self-reflexiveness of his work and his repeated references to *The Nights* in his fiction reflects Burton's views of the Orient.

In addition, Westerners, according to *Orientalism*, define themselves by defining the Orientals. The Orientals live in an exotic world governed by sex and magic while the Europeans live in a rational real world governed by reason. In light of this, Barth's inclusion of references to Shahrazad and *The Nights* with references to Greek mythology, in most of his works, is an attempt to define the qualities of Western culture. The two points of the rejection of the culture of the Orient and the interpretation of Western culture in reference to Eastern cultures have changed in Barth's depiction of Shahrazad and her stories. Up until the publication of Barth's *Ten Nights*, his projection of Shahrazad and *The Nights* follows Burton's projection of the Orient. From the beginning of his engagement with Shahrazad and her stories, Barth has put into practice his lifetime project of rewriting Burton's *Nights*, complete with notes, appendices, and commentaries. A standard device for the composition of these texts was to follow the

---

acculturating from Arab patrimony, insights may be gained into the collective cultural unconscious, so to speak, and the modes of literary intercourse" (122).
[450] Parreiras-Horta 7

idiosyncratic logic of Burton's notes and the mannerisms of his style from the vantage point of a nihilist sensibility that maintains (following Burton's insights) few illusions about the motivations of Shahrazad, Dunyazade, or Sindbad the merchant-sailor.[451]

Barth, therefore, has been seeing *The Nights* through the translation of Burton while at the same time continuing to be violently possessive in his treatment of the classic by insisting on mixing Western references with Eastern references. However, the publication of *Ten Nights* has put a partial stop to Barth's devotion to Burton's interpretation of *The Nights* where the Orient has been seen as exotic and unreal. Barth's *Ten Nights*, reveals a real Orient that is tied to the situation of the 9/11 attacks on the United States.

Also, the emergence of chaos theory[452] near end of the 1960s that has become a prominent feature of the understanding of numerous aspects of life and living has made a strong impact on fiction and on literary figures, such as John Barth. The importance of chaos theory is that it operates on complex non-linear systems that are sensitive to initial conditions. It looks as if chaos theory is tailored for *The Nights* as *The Nights* is a body of complex non-linear narratives. The story of Shahrayar deciding to behead a bride every night until Shahrazad comes with a story that represents, according to chaos theory, an initial condition in the form of a story she will not complete until the following night when another story starts and will also not end but in the following night etc. This symmetrical system of the sea of stories that are dependent on Shahrazad's initial fictional condition is very fit for the application of chaos theory. In addition, chaos theory is important for metafiction as it is a means to find meaning in what seems a chaotic form. Merja Polvinen, in her dissertation *Reading the Texture of Reality: Chaos Theory, Literature and the Humanist Perspective*, discusses the application of chaos theory to the field of literature. Polvinen says, "One of the most prominent characteristics of chaotic systems is that they display symmetry across scales."[453] These patterns could be clearly seen, according to Polvinen, when watching graphics performed by computers where dynamic behavior appears as graphs that can be followed scientifically. Chaos theory, then, is a marvelous tool that makes science applicable to literature:

"Because of this ability to graph complex behavior in geometrical forms, chaos theory has been seen as a tool with which both the details of literary form and even the process of making meaning might be visualized and thus be rendered comprehensible."[454]

John Barth's explicit interest in chaos theory can be traced back to 1991 when he participated in a symposium regarding the direction literary theory was taking starting roughly from the 1980s. Postmodernism, arabesque, and chaos theory were Barth's three main topics of discussion in the symposium. For Barth, chaos theory represents a directing force. Barth "is an author who has found in

---

[451] Parreiras-Horta 263
[452] See above p. 82
[453] Merja Polvinen 83
[454] Polvinen 83–84

chaos theory the perfect metaphor and structure to express what he has been doing for decades rather than an inspiration for something completely new."[455] From the start of his writing career, Barth has been metafictionlly using easily identifiable past time narratives, such as Greek mythology, *The Nights*, etc. in order to create his own new structures.

In Barth's fiction of the mid-1990s and on, notions of chaos theory are related or explained by metafiction. In her discussion of Barth's story-collection *On with the Story* (1996/7), Polvinen uncovers notions from chaos theory she makes visible by pointing out how Barth's temporal structures combine the experience of dizzying speed with arresting passages of metafictional digression, and by suggesting that in his works explicitly crafted structure and the relationship of that structure to reality are central to literary meaning.[456]

In Barth's work, there are, according to Polvinen, self-conscious metafictional structures that give his work crafty appearances; there are larger frames with individual narratives. The individual narratives are digressions that support and echo themes present in the larger frames.[457] Most noticeably, there is an obvious link between structure and reality, which is a new quality in Barth's fiction strengthened by his acknowledgement of the laws of chaos theory.

Barth's new emphasis on the relationship of fiction to reality has opened up his fiction to wider dimensions. Polvinen says:

"The metafictional forms employed by Barth do not serve the purpose of enclosing the fiction in a textual bubble… The analysis of the way in which chaos theory functions in Barth's fiction shows that his extensive play with texture is not done at the expense of meaning."[458]

Barth, in his fiction and non-fiction during the last decade of the twentieth century and on, stresses two points. First, the notions of chaos theory are the very stock-in-trade of late twentieth-century metafiction. Second, these notions are involved in arabesque,[459] and *The Nights* is a precursor to arabesque "as the significant European appropriation from Arabo-Oriental literature and art history is not subject matter but design: 'arabesque' in the sense of elaborately and/or subtly *framed* design."[460] For its carefully designed form, *The Nights* has become even more popular and metafictional with the popularity of chaos theory. Moreover, its popularity has been drawing attention not only to its form but also to its connection with reality. It could be fairly easy to see the connection with reality in stories that mention Baghdad, Khalifah Haroun Al Rasheed, Cairo, Damascus, Basra, or other places and characters related to them. The connection to reality is a fairly new development in metafictional narratives related to *The Nights* in the West.

---

[455] Polvinen 121
[456] Polvinen 122
[457] Polvinen 127
[458] Polvinen 136
[459] Barth *Further Fridays* 321
[460] Barth *Further Fridays* 318

Furthermore, the translation and writing of other works self-reflexive of *The Nights* into French and English, have contributed in giving another perspective concerning the relationship of Shahrayar and Shahrazad of *The Nights*. These works include literary works such as Al-Hakim's play, *Shahrazad*, (translated into French in 1936 and into English in 1945), Ba-Kathir's play, *Sir Shahrazad* (translated into French in 1954), and Mahfouz's *Arabian Nights and Days*, (translated into English in 1995). They also include critical works written in English by Easterners such as Ferial Ghazoul's *The Arabian Nights: a Structural Ananlysis* (1980), and *Nocturnal Poetics: The Arabian Nights in Comparative Context* (1996). These works, along with Said's *Orientalism* and the application of the notions of chaos theory, have led Westerners to view the relationships among the main characters of *The Nights* differently from what was projected by the nineteenth century translations of *The Nights*. In Al-Hakim's play, Shahrayar is unhappy after the end of the thousand nights of story-telling; Mahfouz's *Arabian Nights and Days* has almost the same themes. In Ba-Kathir's play, Shahrayar is impotent and he plots his wife's infidelity to cover up his impotence. More importantly, all these three works can be seen as reflective of the realities of the political and social situations prevailing during the production of each of them. Before the above-mentioned works reached the West, *The Nights* had been seen as an exotic book of fantasy that is not related to reality. After these works, the East is seen as a real contemporary place with inhabitants capable of producing works with philosophical values and personal experiences.

Professor John Barth's literary trajectory serves as an example representing the effect of the production of the above-mentioned Eastern texts and other international factors. Barth's change of attitude can be seen in his fiction and non-fiction works. In his article "The Literature of Replenishment" (1980) Barth says: "postmodernist writers write a fiction that is more and more about itself and its process, less and less about objective reality and life in the world."[461] In his novel, *The Last Voyage of Somebody the Sailor* (1991), which is self-reflexive of *The Nights*, Barth explicitly refers to the exotic world of *The Nights* as his protagonist is tired of being tied to reality and longs for the fantasies exaggerated in the translation of Burton's *Nights*,

"My recent reading in Mrs. Moore's *Arabian Nights* had made me chafe not only at being ineluctably I and here and now but likewise at the iron constraints of nature itself, which made it quite certain that no fish would really ever talk and no genie appear from a bottle, nor would Daisy and I be magically transported from Dorset County to Samarkand or Serendib."[462]

Reality is not sought after; on the contrary, *The Last Voyage* is an escape from reality toward a world of magic where the protagonist identifies himself through the identity of the fictional character Sinbad the sailor whom the West, because of the effect of Burton's translation, has been seen as fictive. In addition to this, *The Last Voyage* "appeared before Barth became consciously aware of

---

[461] Barth *The Friday Book* 200
[462] Barth *The Last Voyage* 87

chaos theory as a possible metaphor for the reflective loop of self-definition."[463] According to Barth, metafiction before chaos theory was experimental; metafiction in *The Nights* is orderly as there are rules to the game.[464]

After the middle of the 1990s, there is a change in Barth's applications of metafictional techniques. His self-reflexivity of *The Nights* in his novel *Ten Nights* is less experimental and more orderly in that it is tied to reality from its start. Barth opens his novel with the following paragraph:

There is meant to have been a book called *Ten Nights and a Night*, which had it gotten itself written before TEOTWAW(A)KI- 9/11/2001—might have opened with a sportive extended invocation to the Storyteller's Muse, more or less like this: "Tell, O Muse of a Story, the hundred-percent-made-up tale of a modern-day Odysseus interlude with the brackish tidewater marsh-nymph here called WYSIWYG."[465]

Barth states that he has intended to write another cycle of 'the art of night'; a work called *Ten Nights and a Night*, but the events of 9/11 have given his intended work a new dimension. His previous plan was to refer to classical works, Western and Eastern, as he calls for a muse, and Shahrazad, the narrator of the nights, was the model for his intended muse WYSIWYG. Also, for the structure of his work Barth borrowed the structure of *The Nights* with the division into nights and the addition of one to number ten. But, his metafictional references are expanded by the phrase, *Eleven Stories*, added to his title in a possibly clear reference to the realities of the 9/11 attacks.

Contemporary Eastern texts associated with the original, *The Nights*, therefore, are, as mentioned above, associated with the realities of their times. They can be viewed as reflective of the philosophical values and personal experiences of their writers. These texts, crowned by Naguib Mahfouz's *Arabian Nights and Days*, are literary works that reached the West and must have affected the production of literature. There is hardly any doubt that Barth has read Al-Hakim's and/or Mahfouz's novels in English, and read references to Ba-Kathir's plays since Barth is a widely informed literary scholar who is interested in 'the art of nights.' In addition, there is no doubt that these texts are parts of 'the art of nights' cycle of stories, and they are metafictional. Mahfouz's novel, as a representative of them, provides a form of reading of the political realities of Egypt at the time of its production as it has a "political thrust."[466] Mahfouz himself supports this fact in *Arabian Nights and Days* saying in an interview:

"I think that in this novel I expressed my fundamental concerns, and that I produced a blend of what can be called 'political realism' and 'metaphysical speculation,' which may be labeled as 'Sufi speculation.' I found in *The Thousand and One Nights* a space which allowed me to express such an admixture of widely separate components."[467]

---

[463] Polvinen 172

[464] Barth *Further Fridays* 322

[465] Barth *Ten Nights* 1

[466] Ghazoul *Nocturnal Poetics* 137

[467] Ghazoul *Nocturnal Poetics* 137

Mahfouz has found in *The Nights* a means he could manipulate to infuse reality into fiction, creating a metafictional setting fit for the literary atmosphere created after the advent of chaos theory and looking at chaology "as an essential postmodern science."[468] Barth, therefore, is keeping with the development in literature, through identifying this admixture through the *Arabian Nights and Days* of Mahfouz.

In Barth's *Ten Nights*, which was published a decade after the publication of the translation of Mahfouz's *Arabian Nights and Days* into English, there is an idea that seems to have come from Mahfouz's *Arabian Nights and Days*. In the original, *The Nights*, there is no hint that Shahrazad, the story-teller, is unhappy in her relationship with Shahrayar after the end of the thousand and one nights of story-telling. "In the course of time Shahrazad bore Shahrayar three children and that, having learned to trust and love her, he spared her life and kept her as his queen."[469] In Mahfouz's *Arabian Nights and Days*, however, Shahrazad is unhappy. Talking with her father the wazir she says:

"May God have mercy on those innocent virgins."
"How wise you are and how courageous!"
"But you know, father," she said in a whisper, "that I am unhappy."
"Be careful, daughter, for thoughts assume concrete forms in palaces and give voice."
"I sacrificed myself," she said sorrowfully, "in order to stem the torrent of blood."
"God has His wisdom," he muttered.
"And the Devil his supporters," she said in a fury.
"He loves you, Shahrazad," he pleaded.
"Arrogance and love do not come together in one heart. He loves himself first and last."
"Love also has its miracles."
"Whenever he approaches me, I breathe the smell of blood."[470]

The above conversation between Shahrazad and her father the wazir implicitly shows the agonies and responsibilities of rulers and those who are ruled stressing that *Arabian Nights and Days* is a novel "with a political edge and a spiritual depth."[471]

Mahfouz, therefore, has knotted his characters, especially Shahrayar and Shahrazad, with great care. Shahrazad's feeling of unhappiness is brought into the novel to support one of the novel's main themes, which is the absence of justice in Egypt of the 1970s. Mahfouz's Shahrazad, according to Ghazoul, cares for the advent of justice in the world; "she manages to tame Shahrayar...but not

---

[468] Barth *Further Fridays* 287
[469] Haddawy 518
[470] Naguib Mahfouz *Arabian Nights and Days* 3–4
[471] Byatt *On Histories and Stories* 168

to change his nature once and for all,"[472] and that pains her. Shahrazad is unhappy to the point of hating Shahrayar for what he represents, which is the absence of justice. Shahrazad's feeling of unhappiness, then, is not a marginal development in Mahfouz's novel. It is an essential tactic move that ties fiction to reality. It is easy to change things around in fiction, but in reality change is governed by numerous factors such as the nature of things, humans, and events. In *Arabian Nights and Days*, those who rule, either politicians or religious figures, are tied more to reality. They err and make wrong judgments because they are humans affected by prevailing circumstances and events. Mahfouz's Shahrayar is a ruler, a politician who makes mistakes that no one questions, and Shahrazad hates him for that.

In John Barth's 2004 *Ten Nights*, the writer Graybard exchanges conversation with his muse WYSIWYG. The muse comments on Shahrazad of *The Nights*, saying:

"Her stories are mainly gee-whizzers: light in tone, heavy on special effects like magic rings and genies in bottles, often erotic and sometimes scatological, meant purely to entertain and keep her audience wanting encores."[473] (6)

The above passage from Barth's *Ten Nights* could be explained in terms of the author's view of Burton's *Thousand and One Nights*. Shahrazad's stories, according to Barth's 2004 work, are sexually loaded magical fictions meant solely for entertainment. Right after the above quotation comes the following passage:

"The girl's in bed with the Guinness World Record serial killer: a thousand innocent virgins deflowered and murdered in as many nights since he offed his unfaithful wife, and Scher's [Shahrazad] next in line if she doesn't get his rocks off and leave him wanting more…she delivers the goods both sexually and narratively; bears the monster three children and then marries him when he finally lifts the curse—despite there being never a hint anywhere that she *loves* the bastard! She's just Doing What the Situation Calls For: telling marvelous stories with the ax virtually at her neck and the kingdom on the brick of collapse."[474]

Here, Barth's work acknowledges Mahfouz's tactic move of the unhappiness of Shahrazad in his [Barth] capitalization of, 'She's just Doing What the Situation Calls For.' Barth here is acting according to his Orientalist view of the East and its past and present committing two mistakes. First, in his *acculturation* of *The Nights* of the past, Barth is *possessive.*[475] He "attempts to retell the stories of this fabulous book by rendering them relevant to here and now, seen from his perspective—America in the twentieth century, the novel in its wane, the author as a middle-aged man."[476] Second, in his dealing with the contemporary rewriting of *The Nights* by Eastern writers represented here by Mahfouz's novel

---

[472] Ghazoul *Nocturnal Poetics* 140

[473] Barth *Ten Nights* 6

[474] Barth *Ten Nights* 6

[475] Using Ferial Ghazoul's term. See *Nocturnal Poetics* p. 123

[476] Ghazoul *Nocturnal Poetics* 128–129

which shows his tactic move of the unhappiness of Shahrazad, Barth completely neglects to mention Mahfouz or any other Eastern rewriting of *The Nights* in spite of the *Orientalism* of Said.

Acknowledged or not, Eastern texts including Mahfouz's *Arabian Nights and Days* have been effective in the direction literary theory has been taking represented in the work of Barth, a prominent figure in literary debate in general and metafictional debate in particular. This book, therefore, is an attempt to include not only *The Nights* but also Mahfouz's *Arabian Nights and Days* as representative examples of metafiction and as building blocks that contribute to the development of metafiction and literary theory. It is interesting to note that the metafictional model that is prominent today is not the experimental one similar to the model of the 1960s and 70s but the one similar to the metafictional model in *The Nights* or it is self-reflexive of it.

With this chapter, this book as a whole is proposing a wider-scope literary theory that stops relating metafiction only to postmodernism of the 1960s and 70s and starts relating metafiction to *The Nights* even though it is not part of the Western literary canon. There is a need for literary theory that acknowledges the literary interaction between East and West; an interaction that positively participates in globalization of human understanding.

Looking at his canon, Barth puts forward his processes of writing fiction right in the open in his non-fiction works such as in his numerous articles collected in *The Friday Book* and in *Further Fridays* and in his fiction, more recently and explicitly in *Ten Nights*. Barth is addressing the reader and self-reflexively using well-known fictions, social and historical events, and whatever metafictional tools might help him deliver his message in order to pull his reader artistically right into the world of fiction. John Barth has a life-long occupation with metafictional writing in his fiction and non-fiction works. It is an occupation that appears in almost all his writing since the beginning of the 1960s; an occupation that takes several forms until it has become similar to metafiction in *The Nights*. From the analysis of his metafictional work, *Ten Nights*, which has strong affinities with *The Nights*, the origin of metafiction and the direction metafiction has been taking becomes more apparent. However, many literary critics refer the beginning of metafiction to the postmodern era of the 1960s. Some of them take the appearance of metafiction farther back to James Joyce's *Finnegans Wake* or to the works of Edgar Allan Poe or even much farther back, but none of them has taken the origin of metafiction to the eighth century, to the time of the first mention of *The Nights* as a written literary work. Barth himself in all his critical studies has never explicitly stated that metafiction can be traced back to *The Nights*. This partially means that the existing trajectory of literary theory should be altered by adding *The Nights* as a corner stone of the whole metafictional construct.

Conclusion

This book is an attempt to thoroughly analyze and follow one literary element, metafiction, as a literary approach in order to show that its roots are located further back in time than what was previously accepted. Through uncovering the metafictional characteristics in *The Thousand and One Nights*, in Barth's *Ten Nights and a Night: Eleven Stories*, and in Mahfouz's *Arabian Nights and Days* I have shown that metafictional techniques existed long before modernism and postmodernism. This book, therefore, is a call to expand literary theory in order to include ancient and non-Western literary works.

In order to show that metafiction is involved in ancient fiction, I have discussed motion in fiction and traced how metafiction developed. When metafictional techniques started to be used in the 1960s and early 1970s, radical experimentation in narrative forms were dominant in an attempt to escape the prevalent linear plot structure. Writers of the 1960s and the 1970s were attempting to overcome the social and cultural confusions of those two decades by concentrating on the process of writing. However, these experimentations lost their vigor because they were enhancing the artificial nature of the writing process; they were far too anti-realistic by emphasizing their linguistic nature at the expense of their narrative qualities. As metafictional practices increased, they changed with the change of the social and cultural situations of the time. Consequently, the metafictional narrative discourses of the 1990s and after appeared less radical and more orderly. Ironically then, works of fiction discussed in this dissertation show that metafictional techniques in works of fiction produced after the 1990s appear similar to metafictional techniques in ancient works such as *The Nights*.

The Nights, a metafiction which has been making a noticeable comeback into the consciousness of readers and writers of fiction during the last fifty years or so, has been a force that prompted me to follow the development of metafiction in the West. I went through John Barth's literary trajectory to locate the type of metafictional techniques he has used throughout his fiction and until his work, *Ten Nights*. My aim has been to point out that metafiction in Barth's 2004 creation is different from the radical and experimental metafiction of the 1960s and the 1970s and more similar to metafiction in *The Nights*. At the end of my study of Barth, I pointed out the influence of Eastern contemporary texts represented by Naguib Mahfouz's depiction of *The Nights* on directing the metafictionality of Barth. I revealed that the two authors, Mahfouz and Barth belong to two different cultures that have been viewing the original *Nights* differently. This difference would contribute significantly to the debate of metafiction and to the influence and interaction that enrich literary theory and literary development.

To further explore the uses of metafictional techniques, I also followed the literary trajectory of Mahfouz from the beginning of his writing career until the publication of *Arabian Nights and Days* to show that there are recognizable shifts in narrative style towards metafiction. I analyzed Mahfouz's *Arabian Nights and Days* to reveal the metafictional techniques in this contemporary Eastern text in order to reveal that there is a form of interaction between East and West not only through the source of metafiction, *The Nights*, but also through contemporary literary texts from both ends to enrich the trajectory of literary theory.

These three texts, *The Nights*, Barth's *Ten Nights*, and Mahfouz's *Arabian Nights and Days*, which are important parts of the 'art of nights,' form the backbone of my presentation of metafiction and they provide readers with a means to see how literary creativity is closely related regardless of where and when a creative text is produced. I also stressed on the fact that the metafictional characteristics in these three texts vary and also reveal the direction metafiction as a literary phenomenon has been taking. The relationship between East and West, therefore, has created a continuous flow of direct and indirect influence and interaction in both directions, which prompted me to propose a change in literary theory to include non-Western literary works.

Sources

Primary Sources:

The Arabian Nights. Trans. by Husain Haddawy. New York:
        Norton, 1990.
The Arabian Nights: Tales from a Thousand and One Nights.
        Trans. by Richard F. Burton. Intro. by A. S. Byatt. New York: Modern
        Library, 2004.
The Arabian Nights. Adopted from Richard Burton's by Jack
        Zipes. New York: Signet Classic, 1991.
*The Arabian Nights' Entertainments: Aladdin, Sinbad and 24
        Other Favorite Stories*. Ed. by Andrew Lang. New York: Dover, 1969.
The Arabian Nights' Entertainments. Intro. by Ben Ray
        Redman. New York: Random House, 1959.
Barth, John. *The Book of Ten Nights and a Night: Eleven
        Stories*. New York: Houghton Mifflin, 2004.
The Book of the Thousand and One Nights translated and
        annotated by Richard Burton. 16 vols. Privately printed by the Burton
        Club, 1885.
Mahfouz, Naguib. *Arabian Nights and Days*. Trans. by Denys
        Johnson-Davies. London: Doubleday, 1995.
Schehrezade: Tales from the Thousand and One Nights.
        Trans. by A. J. Arberry. London: George Allen & Unwin, 1953.
Tales from the Arabian Nights. Ed. by Andrew Lang.
        Hertforshire: Wordsworth Classic, 1993.
Tales from the Thousand and One Nights. Trans. and intro. by
        N. J. Dawood. London: Penguin, 1973.
محفوظ، نجيب. *ليالي ألف ليلة*. القاهرة: مكتبة مصر، 1979.

Secondary Sources:

Allen, Roger. intro. and trans. "*Mirrors* by Naguib Mahfouz."
        Studies in Middle Eastern Literature. Chicago: Bibliotheca Islamica,
        1977.
Almond, Ian. "Borges the Post-Orientalist: Images of Islam
        from the Edge of the West." *Modern Fiction Studies* 50.2 (2004): 435–
        59.
Anderson, Perry. *The Origins of Postmodernity*. New York:
        Verso, 1998.

Araujo, Susana Isabel. "*Marriages and Infidelities*: Joyce
        Carol Oates's Way Out of the Labyrinth of Metafiction." *Women's
        Studies* 33 (2004): 103–123.
Ashour, Radwa, Ferial Ghazoul, and Hasna Reda-Mekadashi.
        Arab Women Writers: a Critical Reference Guide, 1873–1999. Cairo,
        Egypt: The American U in Cairo P, 2008.
Barth, John. *The Friday Book: Essays and Other Nonfiction.*
        New York: Putnam, 1984.
---. *Further Fridays: Essays, Lectures, and Other Nonfiction,
        1984–1994.* Boston: Little Brown, 1995.
---. *The Last Voyage of Somebody the Sailor.* Boston: Little
        Brown, 1991.
---. *Lost in the Fun House.* New York: Doubleday, 1968.
---. *The Sot-Weed Factor.* New York: Doubleday, 1960.
Bertens, Hans. *Literary Theory: The Basics.* London:
        Routledge, 2001.
Borges, Jorge Luis. "The Garden of Forking Paths."
        Labyrinths: Selected Stories and Other Writings. New York: New
        Direction Books, 1962. 19–29.
---. "Partial Magic in the Quixote," *Labyrinths: Selected
        Stories and Other Writings.* New York: New Direction Books, 1962.
        193–96.
---. "The Thousand and One Nights." *Seven Nights.* Trans. by
        Eliot Weinberger. New York: New Direction Books, 1984. 44–57.
---. "The Translators of the 1001 Nights," *Borges: A Reader.*
        Ed. by Emir Rodrigues Monegal & Alastair Reid. New York: Dutton,
        1981. 73–87.
Bradbury, Richard. "Postmodernism and Barth and the
        Present State of Fiction," *Critical Quarterly* 32.1 (1990): 60–73.
Burns, Christy. "Re-thinking Modernism after the 1990s."
        Modern Fiction Studies 48.2 (2002):470–79.
Byatt, A.S. *The Djinn in the Nightingale's Eye: Five Fairy
        Stories.* New York: Vintage Books, 1994.
---. "The Greatest Story Ever Told," *On Histories and Stories:
        Selected Essays.* Cambridge: Harvard UP, 2000.
---. "Narrate or Die: Why Scheherazade Keeps on Talking," Intro. to *The
        Arabian Nights: Tales from a Thousand
        and One Nights.* Trans. by Sir Richard Burton. New
        York: The Modern Library, 2004.
Carmichael, Thomas. "Baffalo/Baltimore, Athens? Dallas:
        John Barth, Don Delillo and the Cities of Postmodernism." *Canadian
        Review of American Studies* 22.2 (1991): 241–50.
Cazzato, Luigi. "Hard Metafiction and the Return of the
        Author Subject." *Postmodern Subjects Postmodern Texts.* By Jane
        Dawson and Steven Earnshaw. Atlanta, GA: Rodopi, 1995.

Chiguluri, Rachel Roth. *The Burden of History in the Contemporary Novel: National Pain and Narrative Techniques.* Diss. Vanderbilt U., 2001. Ann Arbor: UMI, 2001. 3038795.

Christensen, Inger. *The Meaning of Metafiction: A Critical Study of Selected Novels by Sterne, Nabokov, Barth and Beckett.* Oslo: Universitetsforlaget, 1981.

Cioffi, Frank L. "Postmoderism, Etc.: An Interview with Ihab Hassan," *Style* 33. 3 (1999): 357–371.

Colla, Elliott. "Multiplying Mahfouz." Rev. of *Naguib Mahfouz: The Pursuit of Meaning* by Rasheed El-Enany. *SEHR* 5.1 (1996): 6.

Coover, Robert. *Pricksongs and Descants.* New York: New American Library, 1969.

Currie, Mark. *About Time: Narrative, Theory and the Philosophy of Time.* Edinburgh U P, 2007.

---. *Postmodern Narrative Theory.* London: Macmillan, 1998.

Davidson, Michael. "The Metafictional Muse: The Works of Robert Coover, Donald Barthelme, and William H. Gass." *American Literature* 55.3 (1983): 484–6.

Dawood, N. J. intro. to *Tales from the Thousand and One Nights.* London: Penguin, 1973.

D'Evelyn, Thomas. rev. of *"Arabian Nights and Days* by Naguib Mahfouz," 1995. *Boston Book Review* (2006):<Http:www.bookwire.com/bbr/fiction/Arabian.html>

De Ferrari, Guillermina. "Representing Absence: The Power of Metafiction in Jacques Roubaud's *Le Grand Incendie De Londres.*" *Symposium* 49.4 (1996): 262–73.

Dickstein, Morris. *A Mirror in the Roadway: Literature and the Real World.* Princeton: Princeton UP, 2005.

El-Enany, Rasheed. *Naguib Mahfouz: His Life and Time.* Cairo, Egypt: American U in Cairo P, 2007.

---. *Naguib Mahfouz: the Pursuit of Meaning.* London: Routledge, 1993.

Elrod, Page Stranahan. *Something Like Love: Exhaustion and Impotence in the Works of John Barth and Sam Shepard.* Diss. U. of Toledo, 1998. Ann Arbor: UMI, 1998. 9829254.

Elukin, Jonathan. "A Thousand and Two Nights: Review of the Manuscript Found in Saragossa by Jan Potocka." *The American Scholar* 66 (1997): 152–4.

Federman, Raymond, ed. *Surfiction: Fiction Now…and Tomorrow.* Chicago: Swallow P, 1981.

Fishburn, Evelyn. "Traces of *The Thousand and One Nights* in Borges." *Middle Eastern Literatures* 7.2 (2004): 213–22.

Gado, Frank, ed. *First Person: Conversations on Writers & Writing.* New York: Union College P, 1973.

Gass, William. *In the Heart of the Heart of the Country*. New
     York: Harper, 1969.
---. "Philosophy and the Form of Fiction." *Fiction and the
     Figures of Life*. New York: Knopf, 1970. 14–25.
---. *Willie Master's Lonesome Wife*. New York: Harper, 1968.
Georgakopoulou, Alexandra. "Discursive Aspects of
     Metafiction: A Neo-Oral Aura?" *Edinburgh Working Papers in
     Linguistics* no. 2 (1991): 1–13.
Gerhardt, Mia I. *The Art of Story-Telling: A Literary Study of
     the Thousand and One Nights*. Leiden: E. J. Brill, 1963.
Ghazoul, Ferial Jabouri. *The Arabian Nights: A Structural
     Analysis*. Cairo: Cairo Associated Institution, 1980.
---. *Nocturnal Poetics: The Arabian Nights in Comparative
     Context*. Cairo, Egypt: American U in Cairo P, 1996.
al-Ghitani, Gamal. *The Mahfouz Dialogs*. Trans. by
     Humphrey Davies. Cairo: The American U in Cairo P, 2007.
Grotzfeld, Heinz. "The Manuscript Tradition of *The Arabian
     Nights*" *The Arabian Nights Encyclopedia* 4 (1985): 17–22.
Haddawy, Husain. intro. to *The Arabian Nights*. New York:
     Norton, 1990.
Hassan, Ihab. "Beyond Postmodernism: Toward an Aesthetic
     of Trust." *Journal of the Theoretical Humanities* 8.1 (2003): 1–11.
---. "The Authority of the Void: A Kenotic Meditation in Five
     Parts" *Third Text* 19.1(2005): 1–14.
---. *The Dismemberment of Orpheus*. 2nd ed. Madison,
     Wisconsin: U of Wisconsin P, 1982.
---. *Paracriticism: Seven Speculations of the Times*. Urbana:
     U of Illinois P, 1975.
Heckard, Margaret. "Robert Coover, Metafiction, and
     Freedom." *Twentieth Century Literature* 22.2 (1976): 210–28.
Hierl, Ernst Sebastian. *The End of the Road: Nihilism,
     Pleasure in the Text, Postmodernism, and Tradition in Thomas
     Bernhard and John Barth*. Diss. U. of
     South Carolina, 1997. Ann Arbor: UMI, 1997. 9815512.
Hills, Rust, ed. and intro. to *Writer's Choice*. New York:
     David McKay Co. Inc, 1974.
Honan, William H. "From 'Balzac of Egypt,' Energy and
     Nuance" *New York Times* Friday, 14 Oct. 1988.
Hutcheon, Linda. *A Poetics of Postmodernism: History,
     Theory, Fiction*. New York: Routledge, 1988.
---. *Narcissistic Narrative: The Metafictional Paradox*. 2nd.
     ed. New York: Methuen, 1984.
Irwin, Robert. *The Arabian Nightmare*. New York: Overlook
     TP, 2002. *The Arabian Nights: A Companion*. New York: Penguin,
     1994.

Jefferson, Ann. "Patricia Waugh, *Metafiction: The Theory
        and Practice of Self-conscious Fiction*." *Poetics Today* 7.3 (1986): 564–
        6.

Kabbani, Rana. "The Arabian Nights as an Orientalist Text"
        The Arabian Nights Encyclopedia by Ulrich Marzolph and Richard Van
        Leeuwen. 1 (2004): 25–
        34.

Knipp, C. "*The Arabian Nights* in England: Galland's
        Translation and its Successors." *Journal of Arabic Literature* 5 (1974):
        44–54.

Kobler, Sheila Frazier. *Postmodern Narrative Techniques in
        the Work of Nathaniel Hawthorne: Metafiction, Fabulation, and
        Hermeneutical Semiosis*. Diss. U.
        North Texas, 1993. Ann Arbor: UMI, 1993.9401152

Kurk, Remke. "*The Arabian Nights* and the Popular Epics"
        The Arabian Nights Encyclopedia 4 (2002): 34–38.

Lanser, Susan Sniader. *The Narrative Act: Point of View in
        Prose Fiction*. Princeton: Princeton UP, 1981.

Leeuwen, Richard Van. "The Art of Interruption: *The
        Thousand and One Nights* and Jan Potocki." *Middle Eastern Literatures*
        7.2 (2004): 83–98.

LeGassick, Trevor. "Najib Mahfouz' Trilogy." *Critical
        Perspectives on Modern Arabic Literature* ed. Issa J. Boullata, New
        York: Three Continents p,1980. 61–67.

Liu, Kate Chiwen. *De/Constructing National Identity: The
        Historiographical Metafictions of John Barth, Joan Didion and Maxine
        Hong Kingston*. Diss. New York: Stony Brook, 1993. Ann Arbor: UMI,
        1993. 9406890.

Lye, John. "Contemporary Literary Theory." *Brock Review*
        2.1 (1993): 90–106.

Mahdi, Muhsin. "From History to Fiction: The Tale Told by
        the King's Steward in *The Thousand and One Nights*." *The Thousand
        and One Nights in Arabic Literature and Society*. Ed. by Richard C.
        Hovannisian and George Sabagh. New York: Cambridge UP, 1989. 78–
        105.

Mahoney, Blair. rev. of "*The Book of Ten Nights and a Night:
        Eleven Stories*." Oct. 25 2004.
        <http://www.themodernword.com/review/barth_nights.htm>

Malti-Douglas, Fedwa. "Shahrazad Feminist." *The Thousand
        and One Nights in Arabic Literature and Society*. Ed. by Richard C.
        Hovannisian and George Sabagh. New
        York: Cambridge UP, 1989. 40–55.

Marshall, Brenda K. *Teaching the Postmodern: Fiction and
        Theory*. New York: Routledge, 1992.

Marzolph, Ulrich. "Narrative Strategies in Popular Literature:

Ideology and Ethics in Tales from the *Arabian Nights* and Other
Collections." *Middle Eastern Literatures* 7.2 (2004): 171–82.

Mast, Eric Arthur. *Who's Writing the Story? A Creative
Thesis of Metafiction*. Diss. Sul Ross U. 1998. Ann Arbor: UMI, 1999.
1390899.

McCaffery, Larry. "The Art of Metafiction: William Gass's
Willie Masters' Lonesome Wife." *Critique* 18.1 (1976): 21–36.

---. *Some Other Frequency: Interviews with Innovative
American Authors*. Philadelphia: U of Pennsylvania P, 1996.

McHale, Brian. *Constructing Postmodernism*. London:
Routledge, 1992.

---. "History Itself or, the Romance of Postmodernism."
Contemporary Literature 44.1 (2003): 151–61.

Millard, Kenneth. "The Metafictional Aesthetic of *High
Lonesome*." *Mississippi Quarterly* 54.2 (2001):251–61.

Miller, Hillis, ed. *Aspects of Narrative: Selected Papers from
the English Institute*. New York: Columbia UP, 1971.

Miquel, Andre. "*The Thousand and One Nights* in Arabic
Literature and Society" *The Thousand and One Nights in Arabic
Literature and society*. Ed. by Richard C. Hovannisian and George
Sabagh. New York: Cambridge UP, 1999. 6–13.

Morrell, David. *John Barth: An Introduction*. Univ. Park: The
Pennsylvania State UP, 1976.

Mottahedeh, Roy P. "Ajai'b in *The Thousand and One
Nights*." *The Thousand and One Nights in Arabic Literature and society*.
Ed. by Richard C. Hovannisian and George Sabagh. New York:
Cambridge UP, 1999. 29-39.

Moussa-Mahmoud, Fatma. *The Arabic Novel in Egypt (1914–
1970)*. Cairo: Egyptian Book Organization, 1973.

Nunning, Ansgar. "Where Historiographic Metafiction and
Narratology Meet: Towards an Applied Cultural Narratology." *Style*
38.3 (2004): 352–75.

Oates, Joyce Carol. "Plot." *Marriage and Infidelities*. New
York: Vanguard P, 1972.

---. "Whose Side Are You On." *New York Times Book Review*
4 June1972: 63.

Ouyang, Wen-Chin. "Genres, Ideologies, Genre Ideologies
and Narrative Transformation." *Middle Eastern Literature* 7. 2 (2004):
125–31.

Parreiras-Horta, Luis Paulo. *Mirrors of Ink and Wonderful
Lamps: The Arabian Nights in Victorian and Postmodern Literature*.
Diss. U. of Toronto, 2004. Ann Arbor: UMI, 2004. NQ94324.

Penzer, Norman M. *An Annotated Bibliography of Sir
Richard Francis Burton*. London: Dawsons of Pall Mall, 1967.

Pinault, David. rev. of "Naguib Mahfouz's *Arabian Nights*

and Days" Book Reviews (1998): 311–14.

---. *Story-Telling Techniques in The Arabian Nights.* Leiden:
E. J. Leiden, 1992.

Pipes, Daniel. rev. of *Arabian Nights and Days* by Naguib
Mahfouz. *Middle East Quarterly* 2.3(1995): nil. Sep. 9 2006.
<http://www.danielpipes.org/article/929>

Plimpton, George. "The Whole Sick Crew," *New York Times*
21ˢᵗ April 1963: nil. 3 March 2008
<http://www.themodernword.com/pynchon/pynchon_v_plimpton.html
>

Plumley, William. "An Interview with John Barth." *Chicago
Review* 40.4 (1994): 6–19.

Poe, Edgar Allan. "The Thousand-and-Second Tale of
Scheherazade," *The Short Fiction of Edgar Allan Poe.* Annonated by
Stuart and Susan Levine. Indianapolis: Bob-Merrill, 1976. 506–512.

Polvinen, Merja. *Reading the Texture of Reality: Chaos
Theory, Literature and the Humanist Perspective.* Diss. U of Helsinki,
2008. Helsinki U. Print, 2008. ISSN 1237-458X.

Pomeroy, Barry Samuel. *Historiographic Metafiction or
Lying with the Truth.* Diss. U. of Manitoba, 2001. Ann Arbor: UMI,
2001. NQ57515.

Pynchon, Thomas. *The Crying of Lot 49.* San Bernardino, Ca.:
The Borgo P, 1960.

---. *V.* New York: Bantam Books, 1968.

Redman, Ben Ray, intro. to *The Arabian Nights'
Entertainment.* New York, 1959.

Renk, Kathleen Williams. "Myopic Feminist Individualism in
A.S. Byatt's *Arabian Nights'* Tale: 'The Djinn in the Nightingale's
Eye'" *Journal of International Women's Studies* 8.1 (2006): 113–23.

Rushdie, Salman. *Haroun and the Sea of Stories.* London:
Granta, 1990.

Said, Edward W. "Creulty of Memory." *Al-Ahram Weekly
Online* 564 13–19 Dec. 2001.
<http://weekly.ahram.org.eg/2001/564/2sc1.htm>

---. *Orientalism.* New York: Random House, 1979.

Sallis, Eva. *Scheherazade Through the Looking Glass: The
Metamorphosis of the Thousand and One Nights.* Surrey, TW: Curzon,
1999.

Salmawy, Mohamed. "The First Book and the Last." *Al-
Ahram Weekly Online* 815 5- Oct. 2006.
<http://weekly.ahram.org.eg/2006/815/op6.htm>

---. *Naguib Mahfouz at Sidi Gaber: Reflections of a Nobel
Laureate* 1994–2001. Cairo: The American U in Cairo P, 2001.

Scholes, Robert. *Fabulation and Metafiction.* Urbana: U
Illinois P, 1979.

---. "Metafiction." *Iowa Review* 1 (1970): 100–15.

Schulz, Max F. *The Muses of John Barth*. Baltimore: Johns
　　Hopkins UP, 1990.

Scott, Steven D. *When Authors Play: The Gamefulness of
　　American Postmodernism*. Diss. U. of Alberta, 1995. National Library
　　of Canada, 1995. 0-612-06283-x.

Segert, Stanislav. "Ancient Near Eastern Traditions in *The
　　Thousand and One Nights*." *The Thousand and One Nights in Arabic
　　Literature and society*. Ed. By Richard C. Hovannisian and George
　　Sabagh. New York: Cambridge UP, 1999. 106–121.

Sessona, Anna Zambelli. "The Rewriting of *The Arabian
　　Nights* by Imil Habibi." *Middle Eastern Literatures* 5.1 (2002): 29–48.

Somekh, Sasson. *The Changing Rhythm: A Study of Najib
　　Mahfouz's Novels*. Leiden: E. J. Brill, 1973.

Sorrentino, Gilbert. *Crystal Vision*. Illinois: Dalkey Archive
　　P, 1991.

Stewart, P. J. "*Awlad Haratina*: a Tale of Two Texts" *Arabic
　　and Middle Eastern Literature* 4.1 (2001): 37–42.

Stirling, D. Grant. *The Narrativity of Narcissism: Cultural
　　Contexts of Contemporary American Metafiction*. Diss. York U., 1998.
　　Ann Arbor: UMI, 1998. NQ27324.

---. "Neurotic Narrative: Metafiction and Object-Relations
　　Theory." *Collage Literature* 27.2 (2000): 80–103.

Tatsumi, Takayuki. "Comparative Metafiction: Somewhere
　　Between Ideology and Rhetoric." *Critique* 39.1 (1997): 2–18.

Tharpe, Jac. *John Barth: The Comic Sublimity of Paradox*.
　　London: Feffer & Simon, 1974.

Waugh, Patricia. *Metafiction: The Theory and Practice of
　　Self-Conscious Fiction*. New York: Methuen, 1984.

Winter, Benjamin. "The Question of Social Evil and
　　Fractured Truth in the Works of Naguib Mahfouz." 2004. 1–18.
　　<http://www.anythingbinary.net/Personal/seniorproject.pdf>

با كثير، علي أحمد. سرّ الحاكم بأمر الله ـ سرّ شهرزاد. مصر: الهيئة المصرية العامة للكتاب، 2010.

حسين، طه. أحلام شهرزاد. الهيئة المصرية العامة للكتاب، 2000.

حسين، علي محمد. "قراءة في مسرحية سر شهرزاد لعلي محمد باكثير." في الأدب المصري المعاصر.
الطبعة 3 القاهرة،
2003. <http://bakatheer.net/moltaqa_details.php?id=375>

الحكيم، توفيق. شهرزاد. القاهرة: مكتبة مصر، 1934.

طرشونة، محمود. تحقيق وتقديم مائة ليلة وليلة. كولونيا-بغداد: منشورات الجمل، 2005.

قلفاط، نخلة. ترجمة ألف نهار ونهار. لندن: دار الوراق، 2007.

مهدي، محسن. ألف ليلة وليلة. لندن: ليدن، 1984.